AF308017

Defoe
Abbott
Marx
Hardy
Melville
Montaigne
Machiavelli
Chesterton
Cooper
Emerson
Haggard
Joyce
Austen
Hugo
Eliot
Grimm
Stoker
Carroll
Christie
Maupassant
Byron
Molière
Schiller
Wilde
Engels
Garnett
Einstein
Fitzgerald
Hawthorne
Smith
Kafka
Goethe
Dostoyevsky
Hall
Cotton
Kipling
Doyle
Willis
Baum
Henry
Nietzsche
Leslie
Dumas
Flaubert
Turgenev
Balzac
Stockton
Vatsyayana
Crane
Burroughs
Verne
Curtis
Tocqueville
Gogol
Vinci
Homer
Widger
Tolstoy
Whitman
Busch
Darwin
Thoreau
Twain
Scott
Potter
Freud
Zola
Plato
Harte
Kant
Jowett
Stevenson
Dickens
Burton
Hesse
Andersen
London
Descartes
Cervantes
Voltaire
Burton
Poe
Aristotle
Wells
Cooke
Hale
James
Hastings
Irving
Bunner
Shakespeare
Richter
Chambers
da
Doré
Dante
Chekhov
Shaw
Wodehouse
Benedict
Alcott
Swift
Pushkin
Newton

# tredition®

tredition was established in 2006 by Sandra Latusseck and Soenke Schulz. Based in Hamburg, Germany, tredition offers publishing solutions to authors and publishing houses, combined with world-wide distribution of printed and digital book content. tredition is uniquely positioned to enable authors and publishing houses to create books on their own terms and without conventional manu-facturing risks.

For more information please visit: www.tredition.com

TREDITION CLASSICS

This book is part of the TREDITION CLASSICS series. The creators of this series are united by passion for literature and driven by the intention of making all public domain books available in printed format again - worldwide. Most TREDITION CLASSICS titles have been out of print and off the bookstore shelves for decades. At tredi-tion we believe that a great book never goes out of style and that its value is eternal. Several mostly non-profit literature projects pro-vide content to tredition. To support their good work, tredition donates a portion of the proceeds from each sold copy. As a reader of a TREDITION CLASSICS book, you support our mission to save many of the amazing works of world literature from oblivion. See all available books at www.tredition.com.

Project Gutenberg

The content for this book has been graciously provided by Project Gutenberg. Project Gutenberg is a non-profit organization founded by Michael Hart in 1971 at the University of Illinois. The mission of Project Gutenberg is simple: To encourage the creation and distribu-tion of eBooks. Project Gutenberg is the first and largest collection of public domain eBooks.

Sir Joshua Reynolds A Collection of Fifteen Pictures and a Portrait of the Painter with Introduction and Interpretation

Estelle M. (Estelle May) Hurll

Imprint

This book is part of TREDITION CLASSICS

Author: Estelle M. (Estelle May) Hurll
Cover design: Buchgut, Berlin – Germany

Publisher: tredition GmbH, Hamburg - Germany
ISBN: 978-3-8472-2893-6

www.tredition.com
www.tredition.de

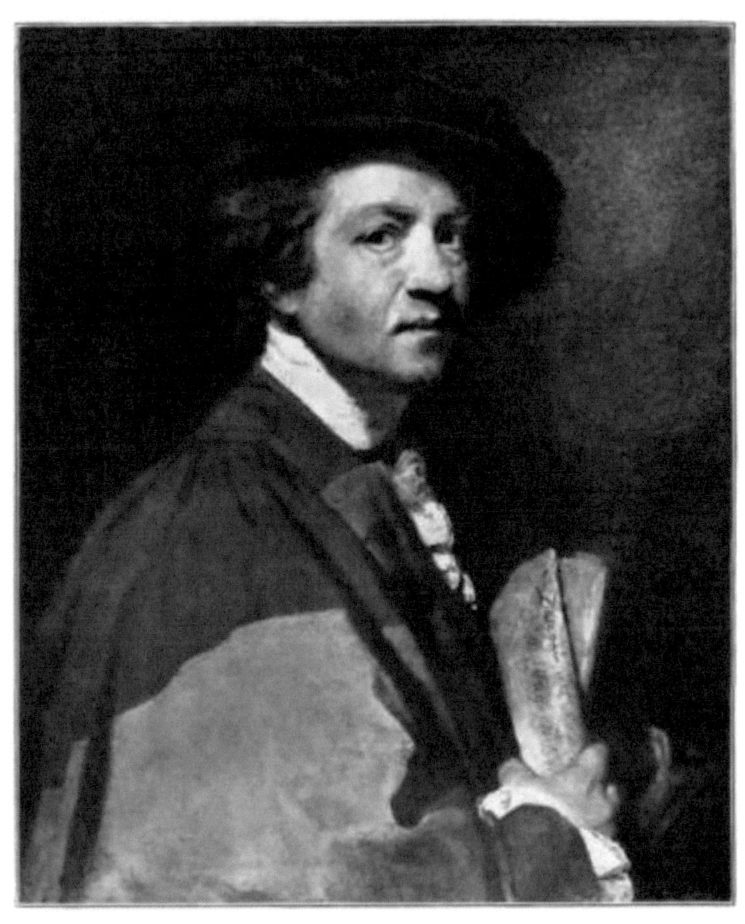

SIR JOSHUA REYNOLDS

Masterpieces of Art

SIR JOSHUA REYNOLDS

A COLLECTION OF FIFTEEN PICTURES

AND A PORTRAIT OF THE PAINTER

WITH INTRODUCTION AND

INTERPRETATION

BY

ESTELLE M. HURLL

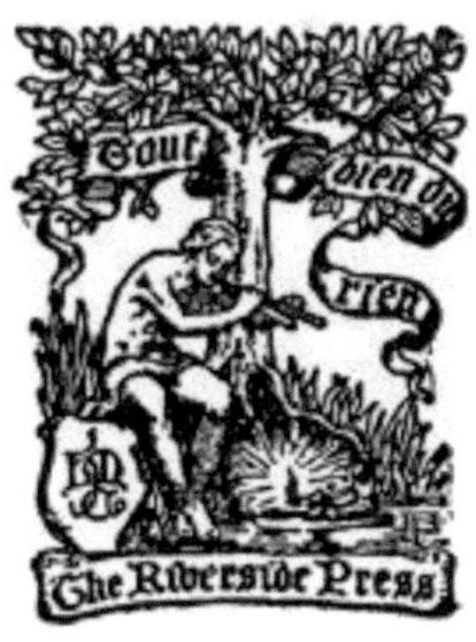

PREFACE

This selection of pictures from Reynolds's works is intended to show him at his best in the various classes of subjects which he painted. Johnson and Lord Heathfield are among his finest male portraits, Miss Bowles and Master Bunbury are unsurpassed among his pictures of children, and the Strawberry Girl was the painter's own favorite fancy picture. Penelope Boothby and Angels' Heads are popular favorites which could not be omitted from any collection. In Lady Cockburn and Her Children, The Duchess of Devonshire and Her Child, and Pickaback we have typical groups of mothers and children. Mrs. Siddons stands apart as one of his most unique and remarkable productions. The other pictures add as much as possible to the variety of the collection, and show something of the range of Reynolds's art.

ESTELLE M. HURLL.

New Bedford, Mass.

September, 1900.

[v]

CONTENTS AND LIST OF PICTURES

INTRODUCTION

I. ON THE ART OF REYNOLDS

The name of Sir Joshua Reynolds holds a place of honor among the world's great portrait painters. To appreciate fully his originative power one must understand the disadvantages under which he worked. His technical training was of the meagrest kind, and all his life he was hampered by ignorance of anatomy. But on the other hand he combined all those peculiar qualities of the artist without which no amount of technical skill can produce great portrait work.

He had, in the first place, that indefinable quality of taste, which means so much in portraiture. His was an unerring instinct for poise, drapery, color, and composition. Each of his figures seems to assume naturally an attitude of perfect grace; the draperies fall of their own accord in beautiful lines.

Reynolds knew, too, the secret of imparting an air of distinction to his sitters. The meanest subject was elevated by his art to a position of dignity. His magic touch made every child charming, every woman graceful, and every man dignified.

Finally, he possessed in no small degree, though curiously enough entirely disclaiming the quality, the gift of presenting the essential personality of the sitter, that which a critic has called the power of "realizing an individuality." This is seen most clearly in his portraits of men, and naturally in the portraits of the men he knew best, as Johnson. [viii]

It is a matter of constant amazement in studying the works of Reynolds to observe his "inexhaustible inventiveness in pose and attitude." For each new picture he seemed always to have ready some new compositional motive. Claude Phillips goes so far as to say that in the whole range of art Rembrandt alone is his equal in this respect. This versatility was due in a measure to his story-telling instinct. His imagination seemed to weave some story about each sitter which the picture was intended, as it were, to illustrate. From Lord Heathfield, refusing to yield the keys of Gibraltar, to little Miss Bowles, dropping on the ground in the midst of her romp, through the long range of mothers playing with their children, there seems no end to the variety of lively incident which he could invent.

The pose of the sitter suggests some dramatic moment in the imaginary episode. Often the attitude is full of action, as in the Miss Bowles, and at times there is a striking impression of motion, as in Pickaback. So strong is the dramatic effect conveyed by these pictures that the figures seem actually taken unaware in the very act of performance, as by a snapshot in modern photography. This quality of "momentariness," as Phillips calls it, so dangerous in the hands of a commonplace painter, lends a peculiar fascination to many of Reynolds's pictures. That he also appreciated the beauty of repose we see in such portraits as Penelope Boothby and Anne Bingham.

Reynolds's inventiveness was so overtaxed by his enormous number of sitters that it is scarcely to be wondered at that it sometimes failed him. Occasionally he resorted to such artificial devices as were common among his contemporaries. Such fresh inspirations as the Strawberry Girl and Master Bunbury could come but rarely in a lifetime. The spontaneity of Miss Bowles is perhaps unexcelled in all his works. [ix]

Reynolds's compositional schemes are of an academic elegance reminiscent of Raphael. He knew well how to accomplish the flow of line, the balance of masses, the symmetry of outline, which produce a harmonious effect. A variety of designs were at his command, from the well-worn but always effective pyramidal form illustrated in many single figures, to those more novel forms he invented for groups such as Lady Cockburn and the Duchess of Devonshire.

Reynolds was frankly a borrower from many sources. In the Roman, the Bolognese, the Venetian, Flemish, and Dutch schools, he found something to appropriate and make his own. From Rembrandt he took suggestions of lighting, and such sombre color harmonies as are seen in the portrait of Mrs. Siddons. Something of bloom and splendor he caught from the florid Rubens; something of the decorative effectiveness of such pictures as Lady Cockburn may be traced to the influence of Titian and the Venetians. Yet to all that he borrowed, Reynolds added his own individual touch. As a critic has said, he was always Reynolds from first to last.

Much has been written of the evanescence of Reynolds's colors. His passion for color experiments amounted to a mania, and cost the world many beautiful pictures. Precisely what was the nature of these experiments, and what combination of pigments ruined his pictures, is of interest only to the expert. Fortunately, enough pictures escaped to show us the original glory of those which have faded. Among the best preserved canvases, "those in which his power and brilliancy appear least impaired, those in which the typical Sir Joshua still most unmistakably shines forth," are Lady Cockburn and her Children, Miss Bowles, Mrs. Siddons, and Angels' Heads.

The range of Reynolds's art is much wider than is commonly supposed. A very imperfect appreciation of his [x] gifts is gained by those who know only his portraits of women and children. These indeed show a peculiar insight into childhood, and a rare delicacy in the interpretation of womanhood. But Reynolds is at his strongest in the portrayal of men. It is by such portraits as the Johnson and Heathfield that he is worthy a place among the immortals.

II. ON BOOKS OF REFERENCE

THE original biographical material on the subject of Reynolds was supplied by his own contemporaries. His friend Malone wrote a valuable Memoir (1804), and his pupil Northcote furnished the first biography of the painter, the Life of Reynolds in two volumes published in 1813. A half century later (1865) was published the most comprehensive work on Reynolds in two large volumes by C. R. Leslie and T. Taylor. At about the same time (1866) appeared a book by F. G. Stephens, "English Children as painted by Sir Joshua Reynolds."

All these books have been long out of print, and there are now but two books of reference generally available. "Sir Joshua Reynolds," by Claude Phillips (1894), is a small volume, but it gives a fairly complete summary of the painter's works, with valuable critical comments. Sir Walter Armstrong's large and richly illustrated work "Sir Joshua Reynolds" (1900) treats the subject exhaustively, and contains a complete descriptive catalogue and directory of

Reynolds's works—portraits and subject pictures—arranged in alphabetical order.

There is an immense bibliography of memoirs of the period of George III., and such books throw an interesting light upon the lives of many of Reynolds's sitters. Some of the most valuable are Horace Walpole's "Letters," Fanny Burney's "Diary," Mrs. Piozzi's "Memoirs," and Wraxall's "Memoirs." [xi]

In addition to these, Boswell's incomparable "Life of Johnson" presents a series of vivid pictures of the life of the period, and contains many anecdotes of the friendship between Reynolds and the great lexicographer.

Reynolds's lectures and writings fill two volumes of the Bohn Library. Of these the twelve discourses delivered before the Royal Academy are the most valuable, and have been reprinted in various editions. The most recent is that of 1891, with notes and a biographical introduction by E. G. Johnson. Intended as means of instruction to beginners in painting, these lectures deal with general principles rather than with practical technique, and are not to be taken as expository in any measure of Reynolds's own art.

III. HISTORICAL DIRECTORY OF THE PICTURES OF THIS COLLECTION

Portrait frontispiece. Painted in 1776 for the Imperial Academy in Florence, and now in the Uffizi Gallery, Florence.

1. *Penelope Boothby.* Painted in July, 1788. In the possession of Mrs. Thwaites.

2. *Master Crewe as Henry VIII.* Painted in 1775 for John Crewe, Esq., and exhibited at the Royal Academy, 1776. Size: 4 ft. 8 in. by 3 ft. 9 in. In the possession of the Earl of Crewe.

3. *Lady Cockburn and her Children.* Reynolds began the picture in 1773 and upon its completion in 1774 received £183 15s. in payment. It was exhibited at the Royal Academy in 1774, after which it was dated 1775. Passed into the possession of Lady Hamilton, daughter of Sir James Cockburn (7th baronet), and by her bequeathed to the English National Gallery, where it hung, 1892-1900, when it was learned that Lady Hamilton had no power to [xii] dispose of the

picture. It was then sold at auction to Mr. Beit, Park Lane, London. Size: 4 ft. 6 in. by 3 ft. 7-1/2 in.

4. *Miss Bowles.* Painted in 1775. Now in the Wallace Collection, Hertford House, London. Size: 2 ft. 11-1/2 in. by 2 ft. 3-3/4 in.

5. *Master Bunbury.* Exhibited at the Royal Academy, 1781; bequeathed by Reynolds to Mrs. Bunbury. In the possession of Sir Henry Bunbury. Size: 2 ft. 5 in. by 2 ft.

6. *Mrs. Siddons as the Tragic Muse.* Painted in 1783 and exhibited at the Royal Academy in 1784. The original work was bought by M. de Calonne for 800 guineas, and finally came into the possession of the Marquis of Westminster, in whose family it has since remained. It is in the gallery of Grosvenor House, London.

7. *Angels' Heads.* Painted for Lord William Gordon (100 guineas) and exhibited at the Royal Academy, 1787. Presented by Lady Gordon to the National Gallery, London, 1841. Size: 2 ft. 6 in. by 2 ft. 1 in.

8. *The Duchess of Devonshire and her Child.* Exhibited at the Royal Academy in 1786. The original is at Chatsworth House, and there is a copy at Windsor Castle, from which our reproduction is made.

9. *Hope.* One of the figures of the window design, New College Chapel, Oxford. The original design was painted in oil in 1778, and was purchased by the Earl of Normanton.

10. *Lord Heathfield.* Begun August 27, 1787, and exhibited at the Royal Academy in 1788. Originally painted for Alderman Boydell, and purchased by Parliament in 1824. Now in the National Gallery, London. Size: 4 ft. 8 in. by 3 ft. 8 in.

11. *Mrs. Payne-Gallwey and Child* (Pickaback). Painted 1779. As late as 1886 it was in the possession [xiii] of Lord Monson, and is now owned by J. Pierpont Morgan, Esq.

12. *Cupid as Link Boy.* The date is not certainly fixed, but it is known that Reynolds was at work in the spring of 1771 upon some subjects of this class, several of which were engraved in the period 1771-1777. In the possession of Alexander Henderson, Esq. Size: 2 ft. 5 in. by 2 ft.

13. *Hon. Anne Bingham.* Painted in 1786. In the possession of Earl Spencer. Size: 2 ft. 5-1/2 in. by 2 ft. 1/2 in.

14. *The Strawberry Girl.* Painted for the Earl of Carysfort (50 guineas) and exhibited at the Royal Academy, 1773. As Reynolds repeated the subject it is difficult to trace the history of the original picture. The painting now in the Wallace Collection, Hertford House, came from the Samuel Rogers Collection. Size: 2 ft. 5-3/4 in. by 2 ft. 3/4 in.

15. *Samuel Johnson.* Painted for Mr. Thrale for the Streatham Gallery, 1772. Now in the National Gallery, London. Size: 2 ft. 5-1/2 in. by 2 ft. 1 in.

IV. OUTLINE TABLE OF THE PRINCIPAL EVENTS IN REYNOLDS'S LIFE

1723. Reynolds born at Plympton, Devonshire, England, July 16.

1741-1743. Apprenticeship with the painter Thomas Hudson, London.

1743-1746. Residence in Devonshire.

1746. Portrait of Captain Hamilton first to attract attention.

Death of Reynolds's father.

1746-1749. Residence in Plymouth Docks.

1749-1752. Voyage in Centurion with Commodore Keppel; studies in Italy; and return, via Paris, to London. [xiv]

1752. Establishment of Reynolds in London as a portrait painter, with apartments in St. Martin's Lane, Leicester Fields.

1753. Removal to Great Newport St.

Whole length portrait of Commodore Keppel by the Seashore, an epoch-making picture in Reynolds's career.

1754-1760. Rapid advance of Reynolds to the foremost place as portrait painter.

1756. Portrait of Horace Walpole; portrait of Samuel Johnson.

1758. Pocket Book gives list of 150 sitters.

1759. Two papers contributed to the Idler.

Pocket Book gives 140 sitters.

1760. Removal to handsome house, 47 Leicester Fields.

First exhibition of pictures by living artists, in room of Society for Encouragement of Arts, Manufactures, and Commerce. Reynolds's contributions, Elizabeth Duchess of Hamilton, Lady Elizabeth Keppel, and two male portraits.

Names of 120 sitters recorded in Reynolds's Pocket Book.

1761. Exhibition of pictures at Society of Artists' rooms in Spring Gardens. Some of Reynolds's contributions: Captain Orme leaning on his Horse, Portrait of Laurence Sterne, and Countess Waldegrave.

1762. Visit to Devonshire with Dr. Samuel Johnson.

Exhibition in Spring Gardens. Some of Reynolds's contributions: Lady Elizabeth Keppel as Bridesmaid, Countess Waldegrave and Child, and Garrick between Tragedy and Comedy.

1763. Four portraits sent to Spring Gardens Exhibition, including "Nelly O'Brien."

1764. Two portraits sent to Spring Gardens Exhibition.

Severe illness. [xv]

1764. Founding of Literary Club.

1765. Lady Sarah Bunbury sacrificing to the Graces, sent to Spring Gardens Exhibition.

1766. Four pictures contributed to the Spring Gardens Exhibition.

Election to membership in the Dilettanti Society.

1768. Foundation of the Royal Academy with Reynolds as president, and honor of knighthood conferred. Four pictures contributed to Spring Gardens Exhibition, September.

Trip to Paris, September-October.

1769. First Discourse as President delivered before the Academy, January.

First Academy Exhibition opened in Pall Mall, April 26, with several contributions from Reynolds.

Second Discourse delivered before the Academy, December 11.

1770. Royal Academy Exhibition in April, with several contributions from Reynolds, including the Children in the Wood.

Visit in Devonshire, September-October.

Third Discourse delivered, December 14.

1771. Several pictures contributed to Academy Exhibition.

Northcote apprenticed to Reynolds.

Visit to Paris, August-September.

Fourth Discourse delivered, December 10.

1772. Several pictures contributed to the Academy Exhibition, including Mrs. Crewe as St. Genevieve.

Election of Reynolds as Alderman of Plympton, September.

Fifth Discourse delivered, December 10.

1773. Twelve pictures contributed to Royal Academy [xvi] Exhibition, including the Strawberry Girl, the portrait of Joseph Banks, and Ugolino.

1773. Honorary degree of D. C. L. conferred by Oxford, July.

1774. Thirteen pictures contributed to Royal Academy Exhibition, including Lady Cockburn and her Children, Three Ladies adorning a Term of Hymen, and the Baby Princess Sophia, Duchess of Gloucester.

Sixth Discourse delivered, December 10.

1775. William Doughty received as pupil into Reynolds's home.

Twelve pictures contributed to the Royal Academy Exhibition, including Mrs. Sheridan as St. Cecilia and a half-length portrait of Dr. Robinson, primate of Ireland.

1776. Twelve pictures contributed to Royal Academy Exhibition, including Georgiana, Duchess of Devonshire, and Master Crewe as Henry VIII.

Termination of Northcote's services.

Election to membership in Florentine Academy, and portrait painted for the Uffizi Gallery.

Seventh Discourse delivered, December 10.

1777. Thirteen pictures contributed to Royal Academy Exhibition, including Lady Caroline Montagu (Winter).

1777-1779. Two portrait groups for Dilettanti Society.

1778. Marlborough Family portrait exhibited at Royal Academy.

Eighth Discourse, December 10.

1779. Designs for windows of New College Chapel, Oxford, executed and exhibited at Royal Academy; also portraits of Lady Louisa Manners and Viscountess Crosbie.

1780. Removal of Royal Academy to Somerset House and exhibition of Reynolds's portrait of Gibbon. [xvii]

1780. Ninth Discourse delivered, October 16.

Tenth Discourse delivered, December 11.

1781. Fourteen pictures exhibited at Royal Academy, including Master Bunbury, the Duchess of Rutland, and the design of Temperance for Oxford window.

Journey to Holland and Flanders, July.

1782. Fifteen pictures exhibited at Royal Academy.

Second paralytic attack, and visit to Bath.

Eleventh Discourse delivered, December 10.

1783. Ten pictures exhibited at Royal Academy.

Visit to Antwerp and Brussels.

1783. Sixteen pictures exhibited at Royal Academy, including portrait of Mrs. Siddons as Tragic Muse, Prince of Wales with Horse, Charles James Fox.

Appointment as Court Painter.

Twelfth Discourse delivered, December 10.

1785. Sixteen pictures exhibited at Royal Academy.

Visit to Flanders to purchase pictures.

Commission from Empress Catherine of Russia for historical picture.

1786. Thirteen pictures exhibited at Royal Academy, including the Duke of Orleans, John Hunter, the Duchess of Devonshire and Child.

Thirteenth Discourse delivered, December 10.

1787. Three illustrations contributed to Boydell's Shakespeare Gallery.

Thirteen pictures exhibited at Royal Academy, including Angel Heads and Master Philip York.

1788. Eighteen pictures sent to Royal Academy Exhibition, including Lord Heathfield and the Infant Hercules.

Fourteenth Discourse, with Eulogy on Gainesborough.

1789. Portrait of Richard Brinsley Sheridan, and "Simplicity." [xviii]

1789. Loss of sight in left eye (*gutta serena*) and abandonment of painting.

1790. Resignation from presidency of Royal Academy and from seat as Academician.

"Mrs. Billington as St. Cecilia" sent with other pictures to Academy Exhibition.

Fifteenth and Farewell Discourse delivered December 10.

1792. Death of Reynolds, February 23.

V. CONTEMPORARIES

Noted Painters:

- Thomas Hudson (1701-1779).
- Richard Wilson (1714-1782).
- John Opie (1761-1807).

- George Romney (1734-1802).
- Allan Ramsay (1713-1784).
- Thomas Gainesborough (1727-1788).
- Sir William Beechey (1753-1839).
- James Barry (1741-1806).
- Francis Cotes (1725-1770).

Pupils and Assistants:

- Peter Toms.
- Giuseppe Marchi.
- Thomas Beach or Beech.
- Hugh Barron.
- Berridge.
- Parry.
- James Northcote.
- Score.

List of Original Members of Royal Academy: [1]

- William Chambers.
- George Michael Moser. [xix]
- Francis Milner Newton.
- Edward Penny.
- Thomas Sandby.
- Samuel Wade.
- William Hunter.
- *Francis Hayman.
- George Barrett.
- Francesco Bartolozzi.
- Edward Burch.
- *Agostino Carlini.
- *Charles Catton.
- Mason Chamberlin.
- *J. Baptist Cipriani.
- Richard Cosway.
- John Gwynn.
- William Hoare.
- Nathaniel Hone.
- Mrs. Angelica Kauffmann.
- Jeremiah Meyer.
- Mrs. Mary Moser.

- Joseph Nollekens.
- John Richards.
- Paul Sandby.
- Domenick Serres.
- *Peter Toms.
- William Tyler.
- *Benjamin West.
- *Richard Wilson.
- Joseph Wilton.
- Richard Yeo.
- John Zoffanii.
- *Francesco Zuccarelli.

[1] The names starred were the artists who formed the first staff of visiting critics.

[xx]

Friends and Acquaintances at the Dilettanti Society:

- Earl of Holderness.
- Lord Gowran.
- Sir Everard Fawkener.
- The Marquis of Granby.
- Lord Eglinton.
- Lord Anson.
- Stuart, the painter.
- Sir Charles Bunbury.
- Lord Euston.
- The Marquis of Hartington.
- Dick Edgcumbe.
- Captain George Edgcumbe.

Literary Club: first twelve members: [2]

- Reynolds.
- Johnson.

- Goldsmith.
- Dr. Nugent.
- Dr. Percy, afterwards Bishop of Dromore.
- Sir Robert Chambers.
- Sir John Hawkins.
- Burke.
- Bennet Langton.
- Chamier.
- Dyer.
- Hon. Topham Beauclerk.

[2] The membership was afterwards successively increased to thirty-five and forty.

[1]

I

PENELOPE BOOTHBY

Somewhat over a century ago, at the time when our American colonies were struggling for liberty, lived the great English portrait painter, Sir Joshua Reynolds. In those days photography had not been invented, and portrait painting was a profession patronized by all classes of people. There were many portrait studios in London, but none were so fashionable as that of Reynolds.

It is said that in his long life he painted as many as three thousand portraits. There was scarcely a distinguished man or beautiful woman in the kingdom who did not sit to him, and many were the children whose portraits he painted. If all his works could be brought together they would form a complete historical gallery of the reign of George III. Here we should see princes, statesmen, and warriors, actors and poets, court beauties and "blue stockings," the petted children of the rich, and the picturesque waifs of the London streets. Among the faces we should find those, like Fox and Burke, whose lives were intimately connected with the destinies of our own nation, and those, like Goldsmith and Johnson, whose names are familiar in our schools and homes. There is something about these [2] portraits which makes them seem alive, something too which gives to the plainest person a certain dignity and interest.

With all the variety of subjects which Reynolds treated he was never happier than when painting children. He loved them dearly, delighted to play with them, and seemed to understand them as few grown people do. In his great octagonal painting room were many things to amuse his little friends, and a portrait sitting there usually meant a frolic.

Penelope Boothby is the name of the little girl in our illustration, and the old-fashioned name is precisely suited to the quaint figure in cap and mitts. We are reminded of that Penelope of the old Greek poem, the Odyssey, who waited so faithfully through the years for the return of her husband Odysseus from the Trojan war. The story runs that, believing Odysseus to be dead, many suitors begged her hand, but she always replied that before marrying she must first complete the shroud she was making for her aged father-in-law. Every day she busied herself with the task, but when night came she secretly undid all that she had wrought through the day, so that it might never reach completion. Thus she prolonged the time of waiting until at last Odysseus returned to claim his wife.

Whether or not the little Penelope of our picture knew this story we cannot say, but it was the fashion of the times to revive the names and legends of mythology, and Penelope was a name which had come to stand for all the domestic virtues. [3]

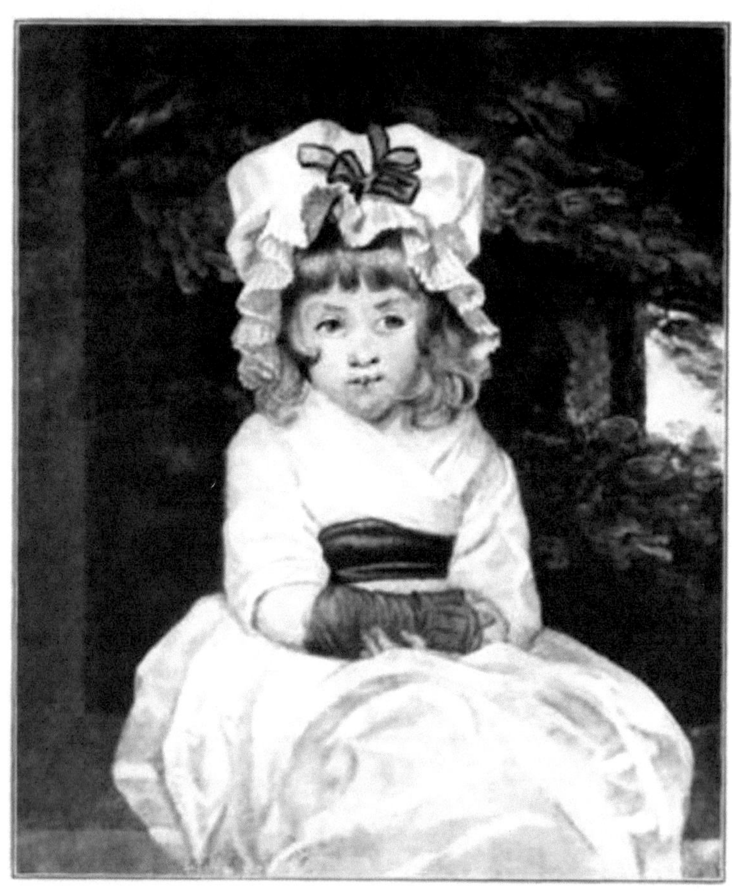

PENELOPE BOOTHBY

Please click on the image for a larger image.

Please click here for a modern color image

[5]

As we look at the picture for the first time the quaint costume of
the little girl suggests the idea that she is dressed for a tableau.
Children the world over love to don the clothes of a past generation
and play at men and women. Miss Penelope, we fancy, has been

32

ransacking some old chest of faded finery, and has arrayed herself in the character of "Martha Washington," as painted by Gilbert Stuart. The snowy kerchief folded across her bosom and the big mob cap on her head are precisely like those in the portraits of the colonial lady. The child purses her lips together primly and folds her hands in a demure attitude in her lap, as if to play her part well, but she is far too shy to look us directly in the face, and glances aside with downcast eyes.

All this illusion is dispelled when we come to study the customs of the period. It appears that children then, both in England and America, dressed precisely like their elders, and Penelope's costume here is doubtless such as she wore every day. A little Boston girl, Anna Green Winslow, wrote in her diary in 1771 of wearing a cap and black mitts which we fancy were not unlike these. There are portraits, too, of other little girls of the time, wearing the same huge headdress, as we may see in the family group of the Copleys in the Boston Art Museum.

Penelope was the only child of Sir Brooke Boothby, and, as we may well believe from her winsome face, the darling of the household. Her home was a fine mansion buried among trees in the [6] beautiful English country. She was, we fancy, a quiet little girl, preferring a corner with her dolls to any boisterous romp, but not without a bit of fun in her nature. She was an affectionate little creature, and very fond of her father, watching at the gate for his return home, and sitting on his knee in the evening. On Sunday mornings she went to the quaint old church of Ashbourne and knelt beside her mother in the service.

All this and much more we learn from a book written by her father which bears the pathetic title of "Sorrows." For little Penelope died at the age of seven, and the stricken parent solaced himself in his loneliness by writing the memories of his darling.

The portrait by Reynolds was made when the child was four years old. After her death, Fuseli painted a picture representing her borne to heaven by an angel. There is also a lovely marble monument to Penelope, by Banks, in the Ashbourne church. [3]

[3] See Mrs. Rebecca Harding Davis's article in *St. Nicholas*, November, 1875, "About the Painter of Little Penelope."

[7]

II

MASTER CREWE AS HENRY VIII

There was once on the throne of England a king named Henry VIII. He was a man of extraordinary character, with qualities both good and bad. His conduct was sometimes unscrupulous and tyrannical, and he let nothing interfere with his own pleasure. Nevertheless his reign brought many benefits to England, and his memory is respected by English people.

In his early manhood, Henry was accounted the handsomest prince of his time, but allowance must be made for the flattery of his subjects. He was a big, rather coarse-looking man, with small eyes, and a large face and double chin. For his noisy ways and rough manners he has been familiarly called "Bluff King Hal" and "Burly King Harry." He was fond of the hunt and the tournament and all kinds of manly exercise. He was also much given to show and display, and loved rich dresses.

He employed as his court painter the celebrated Dutch artist Holbein, who made various portraits of the members of the royal family. There was one particularly fine group which was unfortunately destroyed by fire, but as a copy had previously been made we still know what the picture was like. [8]

Henry VIII. had been dead some two hundred years before the Master Crewe of our picture was born, but English kings are not allowed to be forgotten. Successive generations of children were shown Holbein's portraits of the bluff old ruler, and were taught something about his reign.

It happened one time that the children of Master Crewe's acquaintance had a fancy dress party. The Crewes were people of fashion who entered constantly into social affairs. Naturally there was much discussion over their son's part and costume. It was a happy thought which fixed upon the character of Henry VIII., for the boy's round face, square shoulders, and sturdy frame were well fitted for the rôle.

34

Evidently no pains were spared to make the costume historically correct. Holbein's portrait was the costumer's model, and every detail was faithfully followed. The boy is dressed in the fashion of the sixteenth century in "doublet and hose." This consists first of a richly embroidered waistcoat, the most effective part of the dress. The sleeves are made of the same material and are gathered at the wrists in a ruffle. The lower part of the doublet is a skirt falling just above the knees.

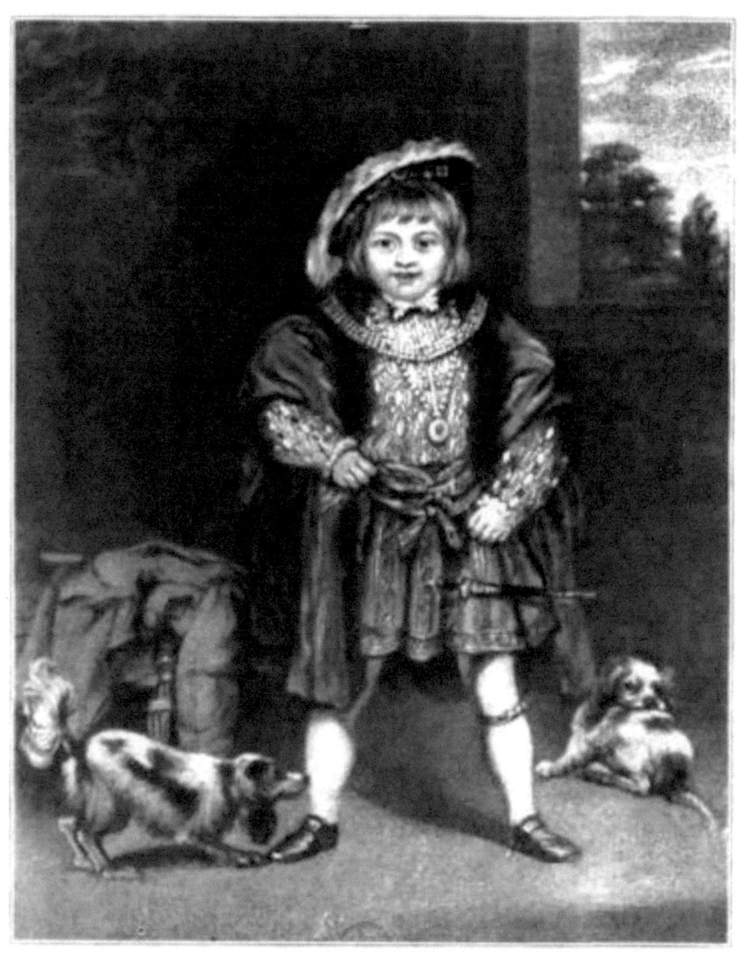

MASTER CREWE AS HENRY VIII.

Please click on the image for a larger image.

Please click here for a modern color image

Over all is flung a handsome mantle; but this is drawn apart in front to display the smart waistcoat to full advantage. A broad-brimmed hat set jauntily on one side, and trimmed with a long feather, completes the costume. By way of ornament is worn a big jewelled collar and a long chain with locket. A [11] short sword swings from the girdle, and on the left leg is the garter, which is the badge of membership in the ancient Order of the Garter, of which Henry VIII. was the tenth sovereign member. This is of dark blue ribbon edged with gold, and bearing in gold letters the motto "Honi soit qui mal y pense". [4]

[4] Evil to him who evil thinks.

It is one thing to have a perfect costume, and another to understand the rôle. Master Crewe not only looks his part, but he acts it as well. He has not failed to take in all the points of the portrait, and imitates the pompous attitude to perfection. He stands with feet wide apart, grasping his gloves in the right hand and supporting the other on the sash.

He is a bright boy, who enters into the spirit of the game, and it tickles him hugely to play the part of a despot. But while he is Henry VIII. in miniature, he is Henry VIII. without the king's coarseness, and in the place is a child's innocent pleasure. It was no wonder that his parents, delighted with the success of the costume, wished to have a portrait made.

The boy is painted as he appeared when posing for his admiring friends. In his effort to assume a lordly air his boyish glee gets the better of him, and he belies the character by a broad grin. Perhaps he has caught the twinkle in his father's eye, or his mother's suppressed smile, and he can keep serious no longer. "Bravo!" cries the audience, and he smiles in innocent delight at his success. [12]

His pet dogs are in the room, and one of them is rather suspicious of this strange young prince. He sniffs cautiously at his legs, for though his eyes deceive him, his sense of smell cannot be mistaken.

Through a window in the rear we get a glimpse of the park beyond, which adds much to the beauty of the picture. As we shall see in other pictures of this collection [5] an interior gives a sense of imprisonment unless it contains some opening. The mass of bright color which the landscape makes in the upper right corner is balanced in the lower left corner by a cloak thrown over a chair.

[5] See Lady Cockburn and her Children, and the Duchess of Devonshire and her Child.

Reynolds painted so many fine portraits of boys that it is hard to say that this or that one is best, though some have preferred Master Crewe to all others. [6] We shall see by-and-by in Master Bunbury, and the Cupid, that the painter understood boy nature pretty thoroughly. This rollicking Master Crewe is not so serious as Master Bunbury, nor so sly as the Cupid boy; he is in fact a typical English lad, sturdy, masterful, frank, and good-natured.

[6] Leslie and Taylor say that "none of his many admirable boy pictures is so consummate."

[13]

III

LADY COCKBURN AND HER CHILDREN

A pretty story is told of a Roman matron named Cornelia, who was one day entertaining a visitor, when the conversation led to the subject of jewels. "These are my jewels," said the hostess, and turned to show the stranger her beautiful children. The story comes readily to mind as one looks at this portrait of Lady Cockburn and her Children. Indeed, the picture was once engraved [7] under the fanciful title of "Cornelia and her Children." Like the Roman matron of old, the English mother gathers her children about her as the choicest jewels of her possession. Her stately beauty is of the classic sort, and the children are as charming as English children are reputed to be.

[7] By Tomkins, in 1792.

All three are boys. The eldest is James, who kneels on his mother's lap, playfully grasping the mantle about her neck, and supported in his precarious position by her hand placed firmly on his back. He has the sweet expression which betokens a sunny nature, and his well-cut features are such as make a handsome man. He was his father's heir and namesake, succeeding him as the seventh baronet.

The rogue peeping over his mother's shoulder is [14] George. Though his features are less regular than his elder brother's, he is none the less attractive, for he is a jolly little fellow. When he grew to manhood he entered the navy and became an admiral. It was on his ship, the Northumberland, that Napoleon was conveyed to the island of St. Helena to end his days in exile. In the course of time Admiral Cockburn became the eighth baronet of the name.

The baby lying on the mother's lap is William. In after years he entered the ministry, married a daughter of Sir Robert Peel, and became Dean of York. It was fitting that one of Lady Cockburn's sons should enter the Church, as her father, Dr. Ayscough, had been Dean of Bristol. Upon the death of his elder brother, the Dean of York became the ninth baronet.

The picture shows the three children in a game of hide-and-seek. George, who is evidently the leader of the fun, dodges up and down behind his mother, throwing little William into an ecstasy of delight. As the round face appears again over the shoulder, the baby reaches up his fat little hand to clutch his brother's arm, fairly doubling himself up in his pleasure, and grasping one foot in his other hand.

James enjoys the play more quietly. It is quite likely that he has been hiding his face in his mother's mantle, but now he pauses to watch his little brother's amusement, his lips parted in a smile, his finger directing the baby where to look.

[17]

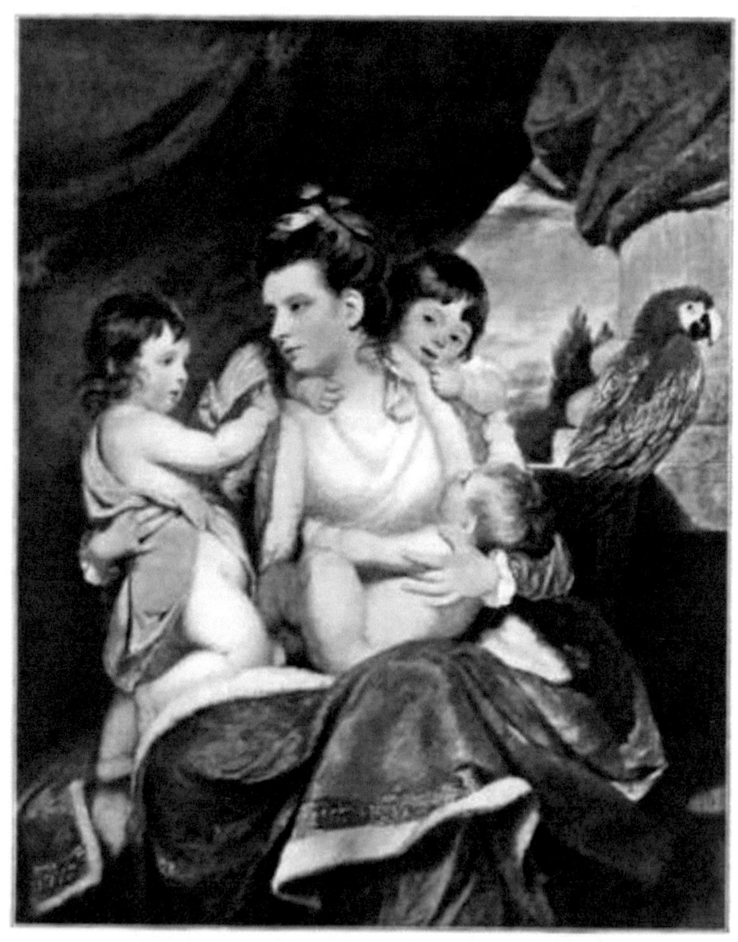

LADY COCKBURN AND HER CHILDREN

Please click on the image for a larger image.

Please click here for a modern color image

The mother turns her face towards that of her eldest son, scanning it closely.

The action in the picture is so delightfully natural that we do not at first realize how difficult a problem is solved in the arrangement of the four figures. An amateur photographer places his sitters in a stiff row and directs them all to look towards a single point. The master artist conceives of some action which shall engage the attention of all, and form a natural connection between them. Thus, in our picture, the interest of the game binds the figures together. The baby lifts his face to that of the mother and brother; the mother turns to the child at her right, and the latter looks down at the baby, thus completing the circle.

The lines of the composition are also so disposed as to bring the figures together in a close unity. Follow the outer edge of the figure of James at the left; trace across the mother's lap the line made by the border of her mantle, and continued along the baby's body. From the mother's elbow move the pencil past the baby's head and along his out-stretched arm till the line ends at the top of George's head, and from this point carry a somewhat irregular line across to the head of James. We have thus traced the parallelogram which incloses the group.

The centre of the group is somewhat at the left of the centre of the canvas, and the picture would seem one-sided were it not for the details of the background at the right. Here the painter has represented a parapet supporting a marble pillar, at the [18] base of which a large macaw perches. Beyond is seen a beautiful landscape. This spot of color brings the composition into perfect balance. More than this, the view thus opened relieves the crowded effect of the compact grouping. The surrounding space would not seem large enough for the four figures were it not for this added depth of space, which gives the eye a long distance to traverse.

The composition is as fine in color as it is in lines and masses. It is a "splendid tawny color harmony, formed by the red of the curtain, the warm flesh tints, the rich orange yellow of the outer robe of satin bordered with white fur, and the gaudy plumage of the macaw". [8]

[8] Claude Phillips.

With so many great artistic qualities, it is no wonder that the portrait has always been admired. Upon its completion in 1774 it was sent to the Royal Academy to be exhibited, and when it was first brought into the room, all the painters present, struck with admiration, burst into a tumult of applause and handclapping. Even after this the painstaking painter probably added some finishing touches and inscribed his name and the date, 1775, upon the ornamental border of the lady's mantle.

[19]

IV

MISS BOWLES

A little girl and her dog are playing together in a wooded park. The place is a fine playground, with its soft, grassy carpet, and noble old trees. It is the sort of park which adjoins country houses of wealthy old English families, where years of training have brought to perfection the trees planted by previous generations. Here and there, through spaces among the branches, shafts of sunlight illumine the shady spot.

The child herself seems like some woodland sprite. She is bubbling over with fun, and is scarcely still a minute. Her spaniel is a gay playfellow,—a beautiful creature, with long silky hair and drooping ears. He is intelligent, too, and devoted to his mistress.

She leads him a merry chase, darting in and out among the big trees which hide her from him. He bounds after her, loses her a moment, and then, as she reappears, leaps upon her with delight.

In the midst of the frolic the child's attention is attracted by a group of boys who have entered the park, all unobserved, and have begun a game of cricket. On the instant she drops on her knees on the grass, seizes the dog, and, lest he should inter [20] rupt the sport, clasps her arms tight around his neck, to hold him fast. The poor spaniel is nearly choked, but patiently yields to the caprice of his young mistress while she watches the game with dancing eyes. From her gleeful expression one would fancy that the winner was her favorite.

Some such simple incident as this Sir Joshua Reynolds must have had in mind when painting the portrait of Miss Bowles; for every picture of his seems to carry a story with it, each one thought out to fit the circumstances and character of the sitter. The lively Miss

Bowles, as we see, is totally unlike the demure Miss Boothby. They are both charming children; but, while Penelope would love to nestle in her mother's arms, Miss Bowles would dance coyly away. While Penelope would sit in doors by the hour, contented with her sewing, Miss Bowles would be skipping about the park like a little hoyden. The picture of Miss Bowles is, therefore, full of action; both child and dog pause only an instant, caught, as it were, in the midst of their play. The attitude of Penelope Boothby, on the other hand, is one of repose, as suits the tranquil nature of the little girl. The background of each picture is likewise perfectly appropriate. Miss Penelope's placid figure is seen against a leafy screen which nearly closes in the picture; but Miss Bowles needs plenty of space for her romps, and has a whole park to herself.

The painter's acquaintance with little Miss Bowles began very pleasantly. Her parents, proud of their [23] lovely daughter, were planning to have her portrait made, and had chosen Romney for the painter. A friend of theirs—Sir George Beaumont—induced them to change their minds and engage Reynolds. Even if the portrait faded in time, as they were afraid it might, Sir Joshua's pictures sometimes having that fault, it would still be more beautiful than if painted by any other hand.

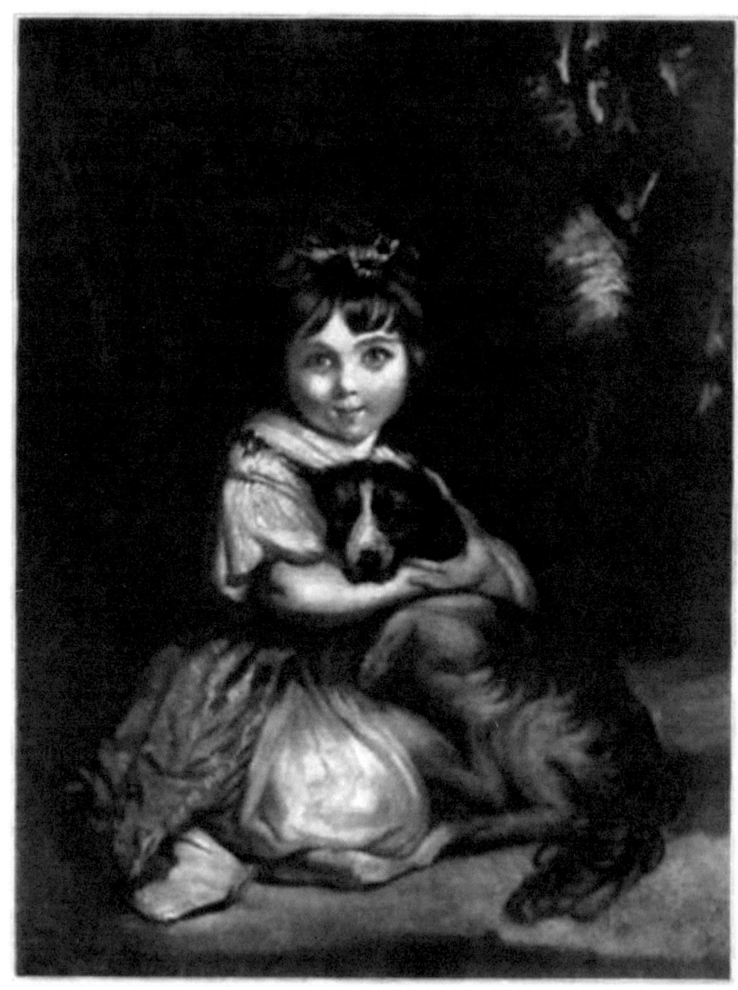

MISS BOWLES

Please click on the image for a larger image.

Please click here for a modern color image

At Sir George's suggestion the painter was first invited to dinner, that he might see the child. She appeared at dessert, and was placed beside the stranger at the table. It did not take long for the two to become acquainted, for the painter immediately began to amuse the little girl with stories and all sorts of tricks. Calling her attention to some object on the other side of the room, he would steal her plate while she was looking away, and pretend to be greatly surprised at its disappearance. They would then try to find it, but in vain, until, when she was again off her guard, he would slip it into place, and there would be a great sensation over its discovery. Was there ever a jollier man for a little girl to dine with!

The next day it was proposed that Miss Bowles should be taken to visit her new friend, and she was of course delighted to go. When the party reached the studio, the child's face was shining with expectancy as she greeted the painter. It was this expression which Reynolds has caught so perfectly on his canvas, and which makes the little girl's face seem actually smiling into ours. [24]

He was equally successful in catching a natural pose, watching her closely as she danced about the room. It was a theory of his that the unconscious movements of a child are always graceful, and we may be sure that Miss Bowles's position here is one of her own invention. Her skirt is spread out a little at one side, balancing, as it were, the figure of the dog opposite. The lines inclosing the entire group form a pyramid.

The original painting is still beautiful in color, being among the best preserved of Reynolds's works. Critics have pronounced it a "matchless work that would have immortalized Reynolds had he never painted anything else."

[25]

V

MASTER BUNBURY

By a pleasant coincidence the year 1768 brought to Reynolds's studio for portrait sittings two young people who began an acquaintance at this time which had a romantic ending. They were Miss Catherine Horneck and Henry William Bunbury, who were married a few years later, and were the parents of the little boy in our picture.

Miss Horneck was one of two pretty sisters who, upon their father's death, had become wards of Sir Joshua, the family being old Devonshire acquaintances of his. They were now living in London with their mother, and were great pets in society. Goldsmith, who knew them well, playfully named Miss Catherine "Little Comedy" from the resemblance between her face and that of the allegorical figure of Comedy in one of Reynolds's portraits of Garrick.

Mr. Bunbury was a gentleman of family and fortune, who had unusual artistic talent. His special forte was in humorous subjects and caricatures, and his works were sought and praised by connoisseurs.

Reynolds must have followed with affectionate interest the lives of these young friends whose attachment had been fostered in his studio. He always felt a fatherly regard for Mrs. Bunbury and a [26] generous admiration for her husband's artistic work. Their elder son, the boy of our picture, was born in 1772, and was named Charles John. The painter visiting his friends saw the child grow out of baby-hood and become a sturdy boy. He was a beautiful child, with large eyes set wide apart in his round face. His expression was delightfully frank and honest. When he was nine years old the portrait was painted which is reproduced in our illustration.

The boy sits under a tree in a pleasant landscape looking intently before him at some object. Though he seems to have been carefully dressed for some special occasion he has been enjoying himself in boy fashion in spite of that. His ringletted hair is blown about by the wind, and the coat is unbuttoned at the throat, as he drops down to rest, hot and panting from some vigorous exercise.

His chubby hands rest on his knees, and his eyes are fixed on something directly in front of him. He does not seem to be a boy given to day-dreaming, and he is much too active to sit still a long time. It must be something very interesting which awakens his curiosity. Perhaps a bumble-bee, buzzing in and out the bell-shaped blossoms of some sweet wild flower, catches his eye, and he almost holds his breath and watches it.

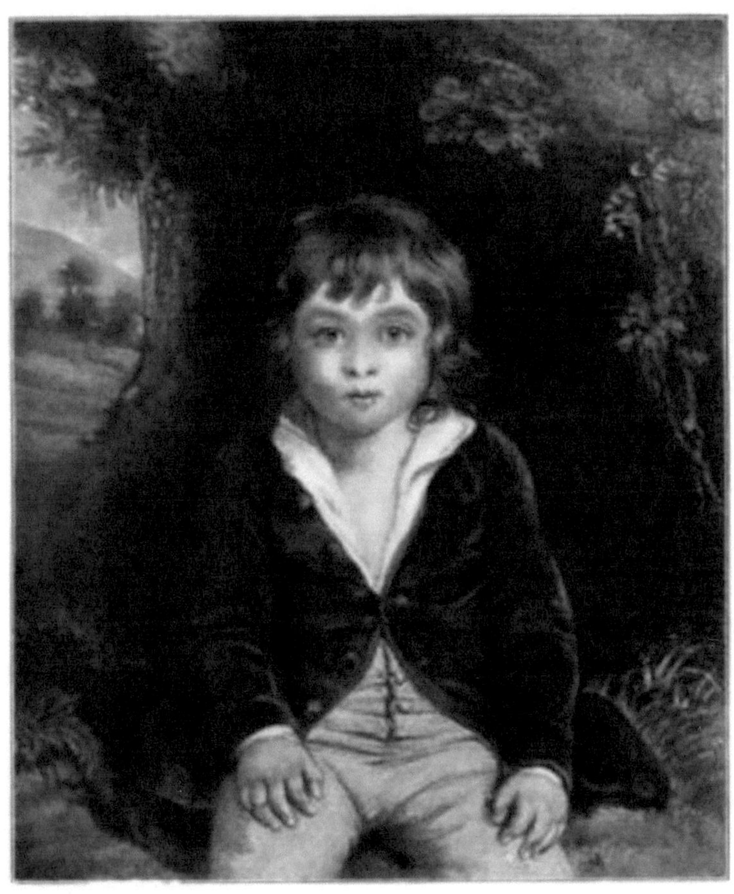

MASTER BUNBURY

Please click on the image for a larger image.

Please click here for a modern color image

The boy's dress looks very quaint to our modern eyes. The trousers and waistcoat are made "in one piece," and the velvet coat, with its wide skirt, seems a garment made for a middle-aged man. As [29] we have already seen, the children of this time dressed as miniature copies of their elders. But while fashions in dress have changed, the child's nature is about the same in every country and period. The eighteenth-century boy, in spite of his grown-up clothes, was fond of all sorts of out-of-door games. Master Bunbury could doubtless match a boy of his age to-day at marbles, tops, kites, battledore, and hop-scotch, and teach him besides many now-forgotten sports, as "bally-cally," "chucks," "sinks," and the like.

The modern American schoolboy, studying the history of our own country, may be interested to know that this portrait of an English boy, who was a subject of George III., was painted five years after the signing of the Declaration of Independence. One of the signers had a son who was of nearly the same age as Master Bunbury, a boy named William Henry Harrison, who afterwards became the president of our republic. If we possessed a portrait of Harrison at the age of nine, it would be interesting to compare the two boyish contemporaries of the old and the new country. Master Bunbury, as the son of an English aristocrat, must needs have re-garded our colonists as troublesome rebels, while on his part young Harrison looked upon the English as tyrants.

Bunbury finally entered the English army and became a general officer. He was sent to the Cape of Good Hope while the British were holding possession there in behalf of the Dutch, and there he died in the fullness of his early manhood in 1798. [30]

The portrait of Master Bunbury was painted a few years after that of Miss Bowles, and Reynolds here repeated the same arrangement which had been so successful before. It differs only in that the entire figure of Master Bunbury is not seen, being cut off in what is called three quarters length, just below the knees. In both pictures the lines of the composition follow the same pyramidal form, and in both also the park-like surroundings extend into an indefinite distance, so that the eye may follow with pleasure the long vista. Both pic-tures suggest the same idea of a child pausing in play to look direct-ly out of the canvas at some distant object. Yet the painter has shown a perfect understanding of the difference in the temperament of the two children, the girl, graceful, quick, mischievous, the boy, sturdy, rather serious, and with a mind eager for information.

The portrait of Master Bunbury was evidently painted by Reynolds for his own pleasure, and retained by him during his lifetime, after which it passed by bequest to the boy's mother.

[31]

VI

MRS. SIDDONS AS THE TRAGIC MUSE

The name of Mrs. Siddons is one of the most distinguished in the history of English dramatic art. For thirty years she was unsurpassed in her impersonation of the tragic heroines of Shakespeare. Her first great success was in the season of 1782, when she appeared for the second time on the London stage. She was then about twenty-seven years of age, and had devoted years of arduous study to her profession. Though gifted by nature with strong dramatic instincts inherited from generations of players, her powers developed slowly. The rôles which she acted were of the more serious sort, which required maturity and experience for interpretation. Her personal appearance was eminently fitted for tragic parts. She had a queenly presence, a countenance moulded in noble lines, a deep-toned measured voice, and an impressive enunciation. In private as well as in public she commanded the highest admiration. Though all London was at her feet flattery could not spoil her. Her children adored her, her friends found her the soul of sincerity, and all the world honored her noble womanhood.

It was while she was still on the threshold of her great career that Reynolds painted her portrait as the Tragic Muse. [32]

In the old Greek mythology every art had a corresponding goddess or muse who inspired the artistic instincts in human hearts. There was, for instance, a muse of tragedy, called Melpomene, a muse of the dance, Terpsichore, and so on through the nine arts. The great sculptors used to make statues of these muses, trying to express in each the highest ideal of the particular art represented.

It was in imitation of this old custom that Reynolds conceived the idea that Mrs. Siddons, as the greatest of tragediennes, would appropriately impersonate the muse of tragedy. [9] The story is related

that when she came to his studio for the first sitting the painter took
her by the hand and led her to the chair, saying in his courtly way:
"Ascend your undisputed throne; bestow on me some idea of the
tragic muse." Whereupon she instantly assumed the attitude in
which she was painted. Among Michelangelo's frescoes in the Sis-
tine Chapel there is a figure of the prophet Isaiah, whose pose is
quite similar, and may have suggested both to painter and sitter the
idea of the Tragic Muse. In any case the attitude which Mrs. Siddons
assumes is entirely characteristic.

[9] Russell had already celebrated Mrs. Siddons as the Tragic
Muse in his History of Modern Europe, and Romney had previously painted Mrs. Yates in the same character.

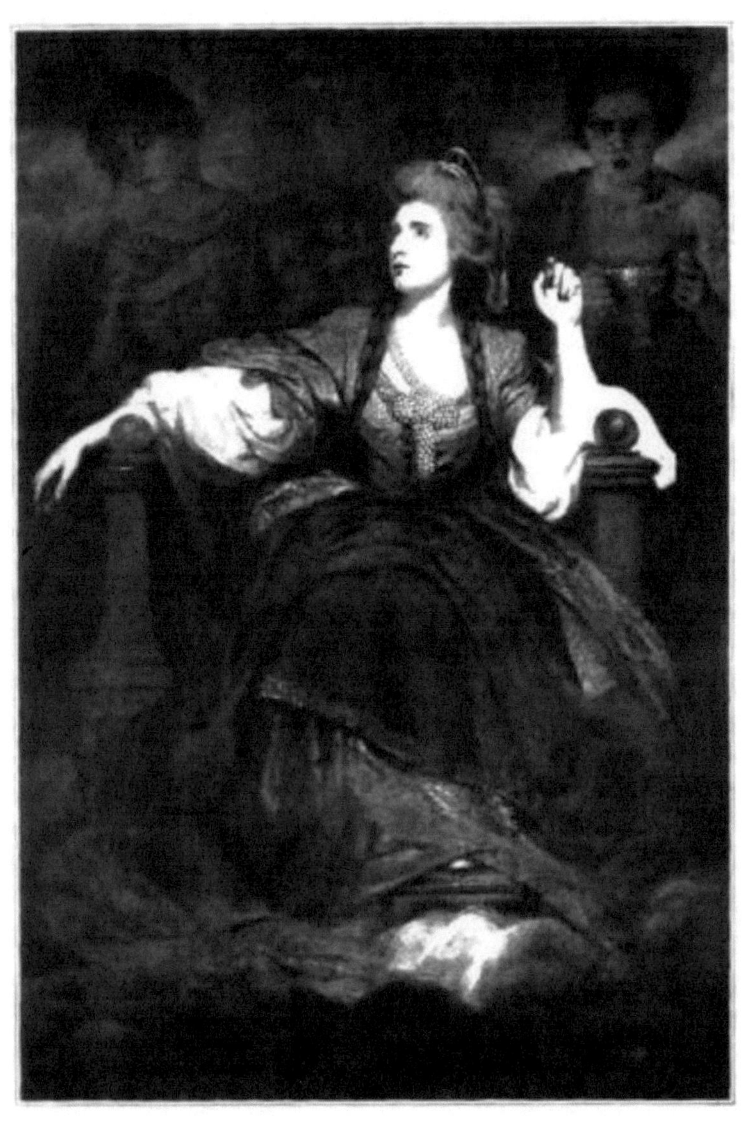

MRS. SIDDONS AS THE TRAGIC MUSE

Please click on the image for a larger image.

Please click here for a modern color image

The expression of her face shows the stress of strong emotion—the struggle of a noble soul in a conflict of forces which must end in tragedy. Her hair is brushed back from the face and ornamented [35] with a tiara like a royal diadem. A rich rope of pearls falls across her beautiful neck and is gathered in a knot on her bodice. A mantle lies across her lap draped somewhat like that in the portrait of Lady Cockburn, and, like it, inscribed with the name of the painter, who gallantly said that "he could not resist the opportunity of going down to posterity on the hem of her garment". [10]

[10] The compliment has sometimes been referred to the portrait of Lady Cockburn, but the incident is related by Northcote as told him by Mrs. Siddons herself in regard to her own portrait.

Behind her chair are two allegorical figures representing Crime and Remorse, the two primary causes of tragedy. In the full face of the one at her left we can trace the features of Sir Joshua himself, distorted though they are into the expression of a criminal.

The color of the original painting has a sombre magnificence which is in keeping with the seriousness of the subject. The painting of the head and bust places it among the finest works of Reynolds.

The portrait shows a remarkable insight on the part of the painter into the character of Mrs. Siddons. She had not at that time played any of her great Shakespearean rôles, but Reynolds seemed to anticipate her power. He followed her career with unfailing interest and always made a point of attending her first appearances and benefits, sitting among the musicians in the orchestra. When she prepared for the character of Lady Macbeth he helped her plan the costumes and sat rapt and breathless during [36] her first performance. This was generally considered her grandest effort, and she used herself to say that after playing it thirty years she never read over the part without discovering in it something new. In this character she bade farewell to her profession June 29, 1812. It was said by a contemporary critic that "there was not a height of grandeur to which she could not soar, nor a darkness of misery to which she could not descend; not a chord of feeling from the sternest to the most delicate which she could not cause to vibrate at her will."

[37]

VII

ANGELS' HEADS

Our thoughts of angels are naturally connected with thoughts of children. Jesus once spoke of the little ones as those whose angels always behold the face of the heavenly Father. Their innocence is the best type we have on earth of the purity of beings of a higher sphere. Often when we try to describe the beauty of some little child, we use the word angelic.

This explains why Sir Joshua Reynolds when called to paint the portrait of a little girl conceived the pretty fancy of the picture of Angels' Heads. [11] The child's fair face suggested that of an angel. She had golden hair and blue eyes, and a very sweet little mouth. It was a face which was so charming from every point of view that he painted it in five positions. Grouping the heads in a circle, he added wings after the manner of the cherubs of the old Italian masters, surrounded them with clouds, and lighted the composition with a broad ray of light streaming diagonally across the canvas.

[11] Originally called A Cherub Head in Different Views.

The child's hair falls about the face in straight dishevelled locks, and it is not easy to tell at once whether it is a boy or a girl. In reality the original [38] was little Miss Frances Isabella Ker Gordon, only child of Lord William Gordon and his wife Frances.

In each position of the five heads the expression varies, and looking from one to another, we may trace through the series the child's changing moods. Let each face tell its own story, and perhaps we may learn something of the workings of the mind behind it.

Here at the lower left side the child suddenly sees some new object, a strange bird or flower, and fixes her eyes upon it. She has a wide awake, inquiring mind, quick to notice all that life has to offer, and she is now in an observing mood. The expression of the face just above is very thoughtful and perhaps a little puzzled. Life brings many hard questions to the serious child, and this is one of the little girl's pensive moods. The two upper faces at the right show quite another expression. The lips of both are parted, and they seem to be singing. One is reminded of the rapturous faces sometimes seen among choir boys when the music lifts them out of their surroundings. All childish troubles and questions are forgotten, as the two faces, flooded with light, seem to look into the glory of heaven.

And now the head is turned and the child gazes directly out of the picture with far-seeing eyes. The expression is of perfect contentment. It will be noticed that the position of the last head is precisely like that of Master Bunbury, and there are points of resemblance between the two faces. The mood and expression are, however, quite unlike in [41] the two children. The boy's eyes are directed towards some actual object, but the eyes of the child here are those of a dreamer fixed upon some vision of the imagination.

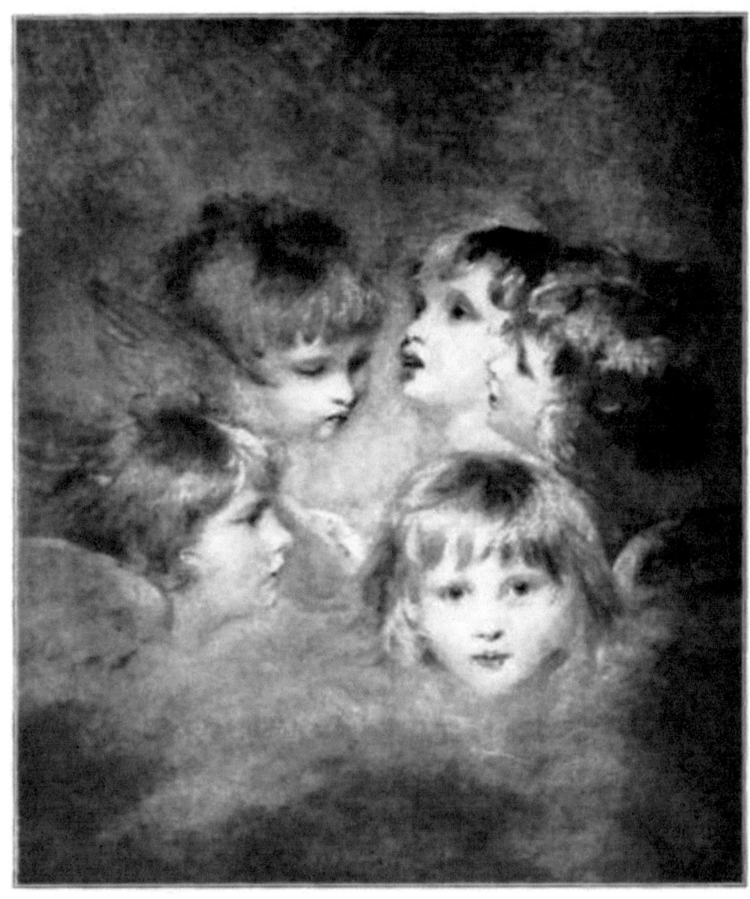

ANGELS' HEADS

Please click on the image for a larger image.

Please click here for a modern color image

A portrait study like the Angels' Heads combines in a novel way the many-sided character of the child. The mother watching a little daughter from day to day feels that she has half a dozen little girls in one. A romp, a chatterbox, a living question mark, a philosopher, a dreamer, a veritable angel, all these and many more change places rapidly in the child's mood. She is taken to the photographer's for her portrait, and the negative shows only a sober little face intently anxious to look pleasant. A more fortunate photographer may perhaps catch her expression of eager interest as some curious new toy is shown her. But that innocent smile of happiness that comes into her face when singing, or that far-away look of the dreamer which she wears in the quiet twilight, is quite beyond the photographer's skill.

Reynolds knew the secret of representing these rarer and more delicate expressions. He was by nature a true lover of children, and many years of experience had taught him to understand their ways. Lady Gordon must have felt rich indeed to have instead of one commonplace picture five of the dearest faces her little girl could show, preserved on a single canvas.

It is true that something of the child's individuality is lost by the sacrifice of the figure. When [42] we look at the other child portraits of our collection we notice how much is expressed in the attitude and gesture of which we here have no indication. Yet the picture shows how truly the face is "a mirror of the soul," and as an interpretation of the child's mind it is unique among Reynolds's works.

The original picture is painted in very delicate colors, and is one of the best preserved of Reynolds's canvases. Miss Frances died unmarried in 1831, and ten years later her mother presented the picture to the English National Gallery.

[43]

VIII

THE DUCHESS OF DEVONSHIRE AND HER CHILD

Georgiana, the Duchess of Devonshire, was one of the most celebrated beauties of her time. She was the daughter of the Earl of Spencer, and was married [12] at the age of seventeen to William, Duke of Devonshire, "the first match in England".

[12] March 28, 1774.

The young duchess was as clever as she was beautiful. She was fond of history, music and drawing, and she wrote verses both in French and English. [13] She was an ardent admirer of the great

Johnson, and in a circle of his listeners hung with breathless interest upon his conversation. Her charming manners, her wit, wealth, and rank drew a host of admirers about her, and she became the leader of English society. Whatever the Duchess of Devonshire did, or whatever the Duchess of Devonshire wore, at once became the fashion. She opened the fashionable balls, she was a leading spirit in the Ladies' Club, and she set the standard for the height of headdresses and the length of feathers!

[13] A long poem by the Duchess was "The Passage over Mt. Gothard," celebrated in Coleridge's Ode to Georgiana.

She was not content with merely social triumphs, but her influence reached even into politics. Her [44] most remarkable political exploit was to secure the reëlection of Charles James Fox to Parliament (1784) from the borough of Westminster. For this she has sometimes been called "Fox's Duchess," but she is usually known as "the beautiful Duchess."

Sir Joshua Reynolds was among the fortunate number upon whom the beautiful Duchess bestowed her smiles. He had first painted her portrait in her girlhood and again as a young wife but two years married (1776). He was afterwards often honored with invitations to her house and enjoyed the hospitality of her brilliant entertainments.

At length (June, 1784) a daughter was born to the Duke and Duchess of Devonshire, whom they christened Georgiana Dorothy. The parents were so happy in their baby that the mother founded a charitable school in her honor. The child was a winning little creature, round and rosy and full of spirits. When she was about two years old the Duchess again called her former portrait painter's services into use, desiring a picture of herself and daughter.

By this time, the girlish beauty of the Duchess had faded, and her slender figure had become somewhat stout. But the new grace of motherhood was now added to her other charms. As she had been the model of fashion for all the ladies of England in matter of dress, she now became a model of motherhood for their imitation. Fashionable women usually gave over the care and nourishment of their children to nurses, but the Duchess of Devonshire [47] took upon herself these tender maternal duties. Thus mother and child were constantly together and became boon companions. The Duchess had a very lively nature, and a child could not wish a gayer play-mate.

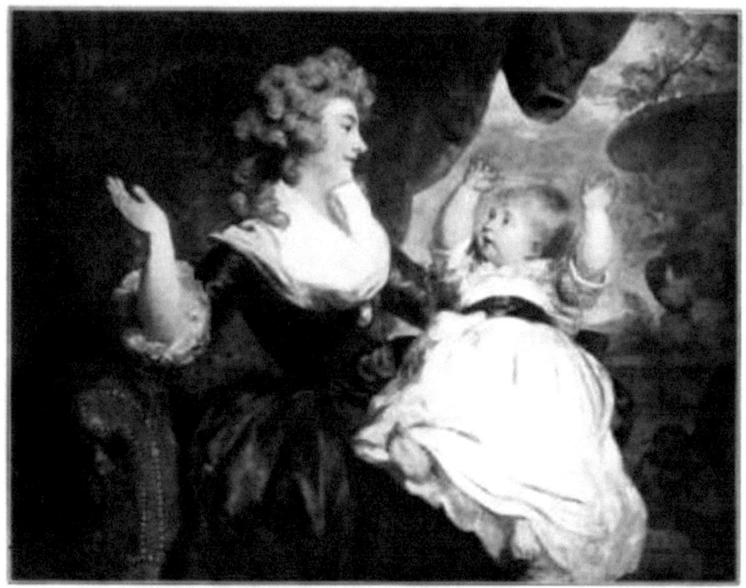

THE DUCHESS OF DEVONSHIRE AND HER CHILD

Please click on the image for a larger image.

Please click here for a modern color image

It is in one of their merry romps together that the painter has represented them. The mother is sitting on a sofa with the child on her knee, and the two are playing the old game of Ride a Cock Horse to Banbury Cross. To and fro on her imaginary steed swings the little rider, supported by the encircling arm of the mother. It is rare sport, and the child kicks her bare feet and throws up her chubby arms gleefully. We can fancy we hear the baby voice gurgling with delight, and the mother smiles at the child's pleasure.

Some years afterward, the poet Coleridge, writing an ode to the beautiful Duchess, pays a tribute to her motherhood which forms a fitting comment on our picture: —

"You were a mother! at your bosom fed
The babes that loved you.
You, with laughing eyes,
Each twilight thought,
Each nascent feeling read
Which you yourself created."

It is interesting to compare the picture with that of Lady Cockburn and her Children which we have already studied. The lighting is managed in the same way, a curtain being drawn aside at the right, that we may look beyond the parapet into the open. [48]

It is an important principle in art that in representing any inclosed space like the interior of a room, there should be some device for increasing the length of the perspective. The imagination delights in distance, and feels imprisoned where there is no opening in an inclosure.

The principal lines of this composition run diagonally from corner to corner, intersecting in the centre. Some of these are so clearly defined that we can easily trace them. One extends from the uplifted right hand of the Duchess across the slanting line of her bodice and along the lower edge of the child's frock. The lines of her left arm run parallel with this. In the other direction the uplifted arms of the baby, as well as the edge of the curtain, indicate the lines which cross these.

[49]

IX

HOPE

We have naturally come to think of Reynolds as chiefly a portrait painter. It was, indeed, by his work in portraiture that his name ranks among the great masters. Yet he made various interesting excursions into other fields. We may see what charming fancy pictures he sometimes painted in Cupid as Link Boy and The Strawberry Girl. Historical pictures he also attempted, but not so successfully. Religious and allegorical subjects he tried occasionally, and it is to illustrate his work of this kind that our picture of Hope is chosen.

The figure is a part of a large decorative scheme for a stained window. The central compartment is devoted to the subject of the Nativity, and shows a group of the Virgin mother with the Christ child in the manger, Joseph and the angels. In imitation of Correggio's famous painting of the same subject, called the *Notte*, the light of the picture proceeds from the Babe. Two smaller compartments on either side are filled with shepherds coming to worship. Below is a series of seven panels, containing the figures of Faith, Hope, and Charity, and the four cardinal virtues—Temperance, Justice, Fortitude, and Prudence. [50]

This plan of subjects was made by Reynolds early in 1778, to meet an order from New College, Oxford, for a window design to be executed for their chapel. Hope was one of the first figures that he painted, and in 1779 he was ready to exhibit, at the Royal Academy, the Nativity, with Faith, Hope, and Charity.

The three fundamental elements of Christian character have been associated together ever since the fifteenth chapter of first Corinthians was written. Artists and poets have had a fashion of personifying them as allegorical figures. Certain symbols have even been invented to correspond to each—the cross for faith, the anchor for hope, and the heart for charity. Thus the imagination has been called to the aid of religion in impressing Christian teaching.

Reynolds tried to put into this figure the various qualities which make up our thought of hope. A pretty young woman steps forth from a region of clouds and lifts her face and hands towards the light. Through an opening in the sky a broad beam of sunshine falls upon her. Following its direction, she seems to be looking through the opening into some glad vision beyond. Like the figure of Hope in Swinburne's sonnet, she

> "Looks Godward, past the shades where blind men grope
> Round the dark door that prayers nor dreams can ope,
> And makes for joy the very darkness dear."

In the lower left-hand corner we may barely make out the portion of an anchor. The meaning of the [53] old symbol is that hope keeps the soul firm, as an anchor holds the ship. The face of which we have a glimpse is girlish and innocent; the figure is full of buoyancy. The left arm and the uplifted hands are very delicately modelled.

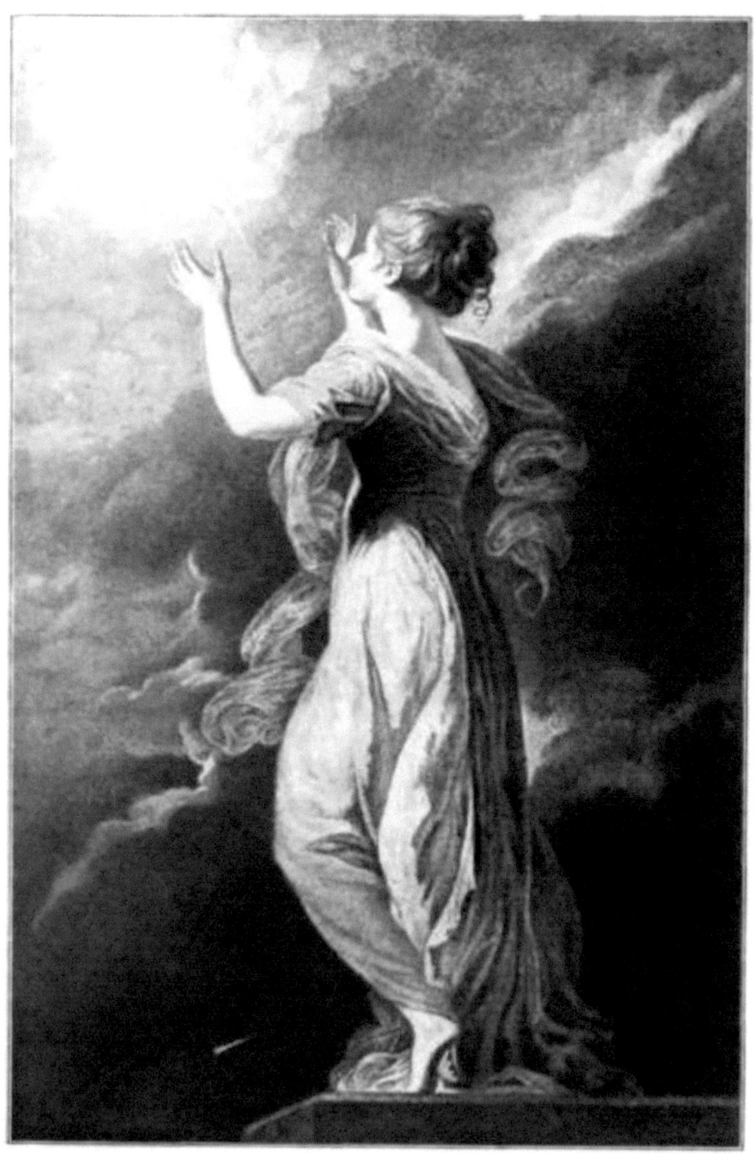

HOPE

Please click on the image for a larger image.

In a painting of this kind the artist is free to follow his own bent in the matter of dress, no longer hampered, as in his portraits, by the follies of fashion. It is delightful to see here the exquisite simplicity of the gown falling in long, beautiful lines. The only adornment is a gauzy scarf, twisted about the bodice and falling on each side in spiral folds. One is reminded of the swirling scarfs in our American Vedder's designs, having, as here, a purely decorative purpose in the scheme. The hair is gathered up on the head in a loose knot, from which the end escapes in a curl.

We are not looking here for any strong delineation of character, as in a portrait, and the painter did not even think it worth while to show much of Hope's face. The panel is to be studied as a work of decorative art, and its beauty lies in its scheme of color, the contrast of light and shade, and the graceful patterns traced by the lines. These are drawn in long flowing curves. The strongest are those which run from the upper left to the lower right corner, to emphasize the motion of the figure towards the left. The outline of the cloud billows which separate the light from the darkness are counter curves cutting across diagonally.

We could appreciate the lines of the panel even [54] better if we could see it in its relation to the entire plan. Each figure is drawn with reference to its place in the great design. Though there are so many component parts, they unite to form a coherent whole, the main lines flowing together in a harmonious unity.

Reynolds's design was executed by the glass painter Jervas; but when the window was set in place it was a great disappointment. The colors are opaque, and can properly be seen only in a darkened room; with the light falling through them they are at a great disadvantage. Nevertheless the window is a matter of great pride to the fortunate college which possesses it. The original designs, instead of being black and white cartoons, as another artist might have made them, are finished paintings in oil.

[55]

X

LORD HEATHFIELD

Lord Heathfield, the original of this portrait by Reynolds, is famous in English history as the hero of the siege of Gibraltar. Gibraltar, as is well known, is that great rock on the coast of Spain, overlooking the narrow strait which forms the passage between the Atlantic Ocean and the Mediterranean Sea. In the affairs of nations this rock occupies a position of great importance, forming, as it were, a "key to the Mediterranean." The Strait of Gibraltar is the gateway through which all ships must pass to gain the ports of southern Europe, and it is therefore a matter of moment to all the civilized world what nation holds possession there. Nature has made the rock a fortress, and military inventions have been added, through the centuries, to strengthen its defences. It has been the scene of some fearful conflicts.

Gibraltar once belonged to Spain; but, by the fortunes of war, it fell into the possession of the English early in the eighteenth century. Various attempts were made to recover it, but the most determined was that of 1779, when the combined land and sea forces of France and Spain were brought to bear upon it. The struggle lasted over three years; [56] but, in the end, the English were victorious, and they have retained the fortress to this day.

The governor in command at that time was General Elliott, who was afterwards rewarded for his services here by being raised to the peerage as Lord Heathfield. General Elliott was already well known as a gallant officer. He had served in the war of Austrian succession, holding a colonel's commission at Dettingen, where the English defeated the French in 1743. In the Seven Years' War he had raised and disciplined a splendid corps of cavalry, known as the "Light Horse."

He was now over sixty years old, and his long military career fitted him admirably for the command at Gibraltar. He showed his calibre in the beginning of the siege, in refusing the keys of the fortress, which were demanded of him. With tremendous odds against him, his conduct has not inappropriately been likened to that of the Greek hero Leonidas, at Thermopylæ, when ordered by the Persian king to lay down his arms. Throughout the defence his intrepidity, resource, and generalship, proved him a man of remarkable military genius.

The crisis in the siege was reached in September, 1782, when a fleet of ten enormous floating batteries opened fire on the fortress, each one manned by a picked crew, and carrying from ten to eighteen guns. These batteries were the invention of the most skilled French engineers, and were believed to be impenetrable to shot. The cannonading began in the morning and continued all day. Soon after midnight [59] nine ships were on fire, and the hostile fleet was doomed.

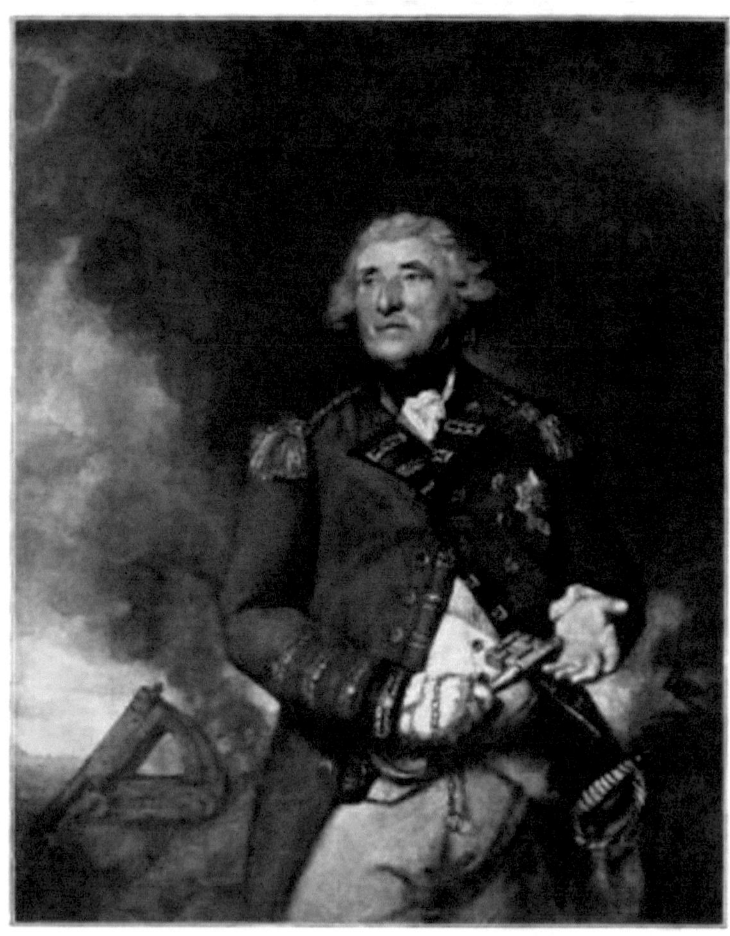

LORD HEATHFIELD

Please click on the image for a larger image.

Please click here for a modern color image

General Elliott showed himself a generous victor, and the men saved from the enemy's ships owed their lives to him. Five years later the returned hero, now become Lord Heathfield, sat to Reynolds for his portrait, ordered by a wealthy admirer—the public-spirited Alderman Boydell. The picture shows the brave old soldier as he took his stand in command of Gibraltar. Some one has said that it tells the whole story of the siege.

The general grasps firmly the key of the fortress, the chain wound twice about his hand, to emphasize the determination of the man to hold it against all odds. His sword swings at his side, ready for instant use; a cannon in the rear is pointed downward towards the hostile fleet, and the smoke of battle rolls in clouds behind him. Far away on the horizon a glimmer of light shines on the distant sea.

The veteran stands as immovable as a Stonewall Jackson. His face is set in determined lines, the lips firmly closed, the head thrown back a little, and the eyes steadily fixed on the battle. Yet the face is not altogether stern; there is much that is kindly and noble in the expression. One can fancy it in another moment softening into an expression of gentleness.

It was a remarkable feature of his success during these terrible months of siege, that he was able to hold the love and loyalty of his men. When the spirits of the little garrison flagged, under the com [60] bined influence of disease and impending famine, his genial presence animated them with fresh hope. His chivalry was as unfailing as his bravery. It is said that "his military skill and moral courage place him among the best soldiers and noblest men Europe produced in the eighteenth century."

The portrait painter makes us feel all this in his picture. The attitude is so dignified, the gesture so forcible, the countenance so expressive, that we are impressed at once with the dignity of his character. Even if we knew nothing of his history we should still be sure that this is a great man.

The last days of the hero of Gibraltar were spent at his home, Kalkofen, near Aix-la-Chapelle, where he died, July 6, 1790, in the seventy-third year of his age.

[61]

XI

MRS. PAYNE-GALLWEY AND HER CHILD (PICKABACK)

Pickaback is one of the old, old games which no one is so foolish as to try to trace to its origin. We may well believe that there was never a time when mothers did not trot their children on their knees and carry them on their backs. The very names we give these childish games were used in England more than a century ago.

The picture of Mrs. Payne-Gallwey and her child has long been known as Pickaback, and will always be so called by many who would not be at the pains to remember the lady's name. It is one of those portraits in which the painter, impatient of the stiff conventional attitudes which were in vogue in his day, drew his inspiration from a simple homely theme of daily life.

What an ingenious painter Reynolds was, we learn more and more as we examine one picture after another and compare them with those of his predecessors. He liked to have his pictures tell stories, and often, when he had a mother and child to paint, he represented them as playing together just as they might have done every day in their own nursery or garden. [14] The Duchess of Devonshire is seen in her [62] boudoir trotting her baby to Banbury Cross, and the Cockburn children are surprised in a game of hide-and-seek on their mother's lap.

[14] Claude Phillips refers to Pickaback as "one of the most popular and representative" of this class.

Mrs. Payne-Gallwey seems to have just caught her little girl up on her back and to be starting off to give her a ride. Her body is bent slightly forward in the attitude of one walking with a burden, and we almost seem to see her move. It is as if in another moment they would pass across the canvas and out of our sight.

The incident is so precisely like something which happens every day that we might think the picture was painted yesterday instead of in 1779, were it not for the few signs which indicate its date. For one thing, the lady's hair is arranged over a high cushion in the peculiar style affected at this period in fashionable circles. The style was carried to absurd extremes, ladies vying with one another in the height of the coiffure until in some cases it actually towered a foot and a half in height. Over this structure were worn nodding plumes of feathers, increasing the fantastic effect.

We may imagine how these unsightly erections vexed the artistic soul of Sir Joshua Reynolds. He was, however, enough of an autocrat to take liberties with the fashions. When obliged to paint the portrait of a lady with a "head" (for so the coiffure was called) he always managed to modify its height and make its outlines harmonize with his composition.

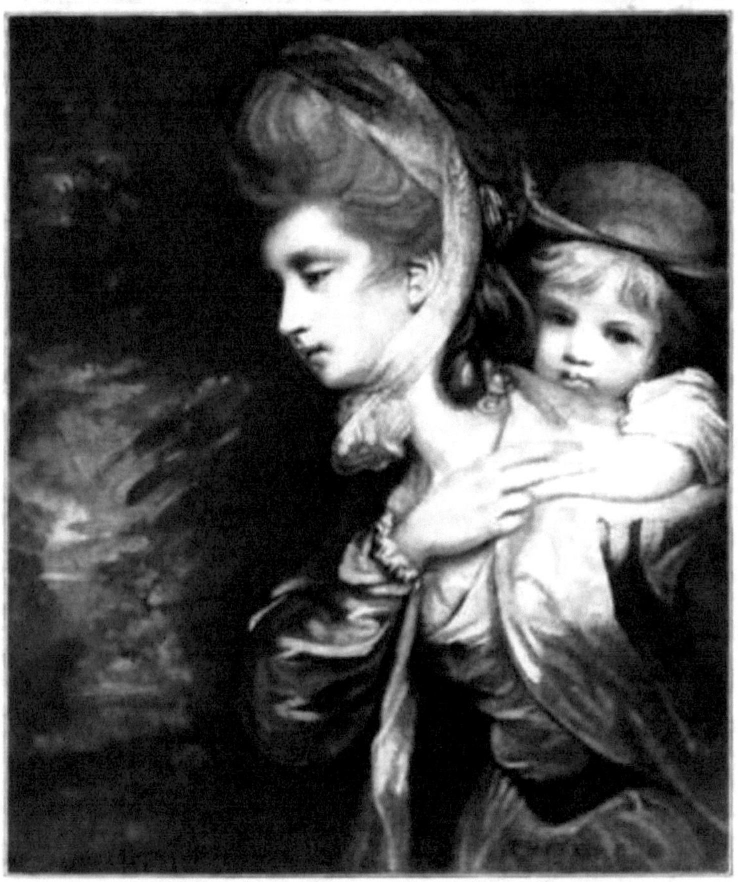

MRS. PAYNE-GALLWEY AND HER CHILD "PICKABACK"

Please click on the image for a larger image.

A side view was of course much less objectionable [65] than the full front, in which the face was elongated to such strange proportions. In this case the face is turned in profile, and its delicacy is enhanced rather than injured by the masses of hair which frame it. The hair, instead of being drawn tightly back from the forehead in the ordinary way, waves in graceful curves, which are quite beyond the art of any hairdresser. Finally, the massive effect of the hair is broken by the narrow scarf bound about it and tied under the chin. The curve of this scarf meets the curve of the profile to form a beautiful oval.

The quaintest touch in the picture is the child's big hat. The same shape is worn to-day by men, and one might fancy that the baby had borrowed her papa's hat for the frolic. It is a curious change in fashions which transfers any part of a little girl's wardrobe to that of a grown man.

We may feel a little better acquainted with the mother and daughter to know their names. Mrs. Payne-Gallwey was Philadelphia, the daughter of General De Lancey, Lieutenant Governor of New York. The child was Charlotte, who afterwards married John Moseley. Mrs. Gallwey's beauty is of a very fragile type, and her eyes have a languor hinting of invalidism. Only a few years later she died, while still in her young motherhood. Little Charlotte has a round healthy face, but it is a little sober. Indeed, both mother and child seem to be of a rather dreamy, poetic temperament. Their mood is hardly merry enough for such a game, but they [66] enjoy it in their own way with quiet contentment. It is an idealized version of the ordinary romping game of Pickaback.

The composition is based on lines which cut the canvas diagonally. In one direction is the line running the length of the profile and continued along the bodice. Crossing this at right angles is the shorter line made by the two arms. It is the first of these which gives character to the picture and produces the impression of motion which is so striking. It is almost as if a modern photographer had taken a snap shot of a figure in the act of walking. But in no such photograph, it is safe to say, would the lines chance to flow in such perfect rhythm.

70

XII

CUPID AS LINK BOY

A familiar figure in classic mythology was that of the little god of love, Cupid. He was the son of Venus, and, like her, was concerned in the affairs of the heart. Ancient art represented him as a beautiful naked boy with wings, carrying a bow and quiver of arrows, and sometimes a burning torch. The torch was to kindle the flame of love, and the arrows were to pierce the heart with the tender passion. These missiles were made at the forge of Vulcan, where Venus first imbued them with honey, after which Cupid, the mischievous fellow, tinged them with gall. Thus it was that the wounds they inflicted were at once sweet and painful. [15]

[15] Anacreon's Ode XXXIII. in Moore's translation.

Now Cupid was always bent upon some of his naughty pranks. He was afraid of nothing, and we read of his riding on the backs of lions and sporting with the monsters of the deep. He played all sorts of tricks on the gods, stealing the arms of Hercules, and even breaking the thunderbolts of Jove. His bow and arrows were a source of great amusement to him. He delighted in taking aim at unsuspecting mortals, and his random shots often wrought sad havoc. [68]

One of Anacreon's odes relates how the poet was awakened on a rainy midnight by the cry of a child begging shelter. The little waif proved to be Cupid in disguise. After being warmed and dried by the fire, the boy artfully craved permission to try his bow, to see if the rain had injured its elasticity. The arrow flew straight at the poet's heart with a sweet pain, and away flew Cupid laughing gayly at his exploit. [16]

[16] Anacreon's Ode XXVIII. in Moore's translation.

Cupid was naturally a very popular god, yet his tricksy ways caused him to be looked upon with suspicion. Every one was anxious to stand well with him. In some of the cities of ancient Greece, as Sparta and Athens, he was worshipped with great solemnity, and every five years festivals were held in his honor.

In our picture the painter has represented the little torch-bearing god disguised as a link boy. He is dressed in the clothes of a London street urchin, and behind him are the warehouses of the great city.

The link bearer's occupation was abandoned so long ago that it needs a word of explanation. In the old times, before there were stationary street lights of any kind, men and boys used to run about by night, carrying torches or links, as they were called, to lighten the way for passers-by.

They were like the newsboys of to-day, running up to each wayfarer to offer their services, and always glad to pick up a few pennies. They accompanied parties home from the clubs, the theatres, and all [71] sorts of entertainments, running beside carriages, as well as foot passengers. Nor was their occupation solely by night. There sometimes came suddenly in London a thick fog, shutting out the sunlight as completely as if it had been night. People caught in the streets at such times soon lost their way, and the services of the link boy were then very useful.

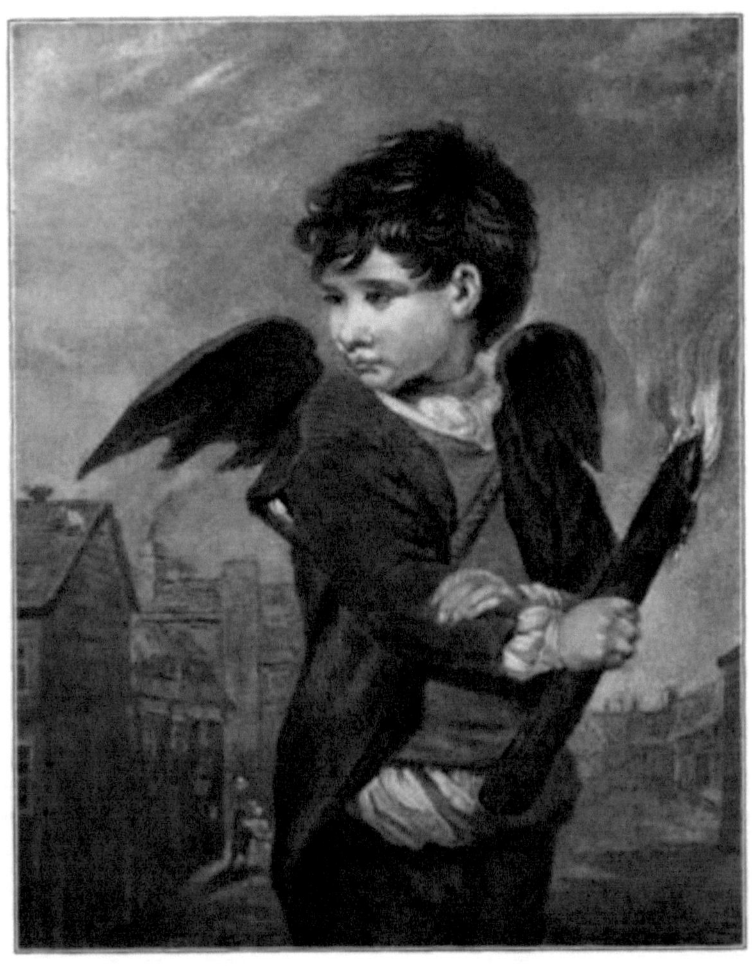

CUPID AS LINK BOY

Please click on the image for a larger image.

Please click here for a modern color image

We may now understand what a capital chance for fun Cupid would have, playing the part of a link boy. The strangers whom he guided on their way would little suspect that the link boy's torch was kindling the flame of love within them. He might lead them whither he pleased, and finally, disclosing his true identity, would draw his bow upon them and leave them to their fate.

It is perhaps after some such escapade as this that we see him in the picture, link in hand, pausing to look back with a smile of suppressed amusement at some of his victims. It seems very odd to find Cupid in such surroundings, and especially to see the little god hampered by the clumsy garments of mortals. They are old and ragged, the cast-off finery such as is picked up by street gamins. The child's hair is tossed about his head in unkempt locks, and altogether he looks the part to perfection.

Yet there are unmistakable signs of his identity in the wings spread from his shoulders. If you look closely, too, you can see through the rip in his sleeve the quiver of arrows which the sly fellow thought to hide under his coat. The face and expression could belong alone to Cupid. The mouth is shaped in a [72] genuine Cupid's bow, and the pointed chin shows his astuteness. Mischief lurks in the corners of the eyes and in the curve of his mouth.

The Cupid as Link Boy is one of a number of fancy pictures which Sir Joshua Reynolds painted for his own pleasure. His portrait orders were nearly all from the wealthy and aristocratic classes, and the artist would not have been content without a greater variety of subjects than this work afforded. He had a fertile imagination for ideal or "fancy" subjects, particularly for those of a humorous nature. Often when he chanced to be driving through the streets his attention would be attracted by some little waif, and he would take the child back to his studio for a model. Our picture is from one of these mischievous London street boys, whose face reappears in several other works.

[73]

XIII

THE HON. ANNE BINGHAM

Miss Anne Bingham was one of the many aristocratic ladies whose portraits Reynolds painted, and one of the most interesting of this class of sitters. Her vivacious face looking into ours wins us at once, and we should be glad to know more of the charming original.

Anne Bingham was the youngest daughter of Sir Charles Bingham, who in 1776 was created Baron Lucan. Her mother, Lady Lucan, was a remarkably talented woman, trying her hand with success at modelling, painting, and poetry. She was ambitious to be an intellectual leader, and like several other ladies of the time entertained after the fashion of the French salons, inviting people of wit and learning to meet in her drawing-room for discussion. Her artistic work was really remarkable. Encouraged by the advice and help of Horace Walpole, she became a skilful copyist, and it is said imitated the works of some earlier painters with a genius that fairly depreciated the originals!

It was thus in exceptionally artistic and intellectual surroundings that Anne grew out of girlhood. Her oldest sister, Lavinia, who afterwards became Countess Spencer, inherited the mother's artistic [74] tastes, and was likewise a favorite with Horace Walpole.

The two daughters were both charming in appearance, and there was a certain sisterly resemblance between them. If Lavinia's eyes were a bit more sparkling, judged by the portraits, Anne's mouth was smaller and more daintily modelled. As a frequent guest in their mother's drawing-room, Sir Joshua must have known both the young ladies. Of the elder he painted several portraits; of the younger, but this one, executed in 1786.

It was a natural and appropriate idea that Miss Anne's portrait should be made in a style similar to one of her sister, as a companion picture. Both were represented in half-length figure, wearing white kerchiefs and broad-brimmed hats.

Those must have been pleasant sittings which gave the veteran portrait painter Miss Anne for a subject. [17] Plainly there was a perfect sympathy between sitter and painter. The smile the lady turns towards the easel is as naïve as that of Miss Bowles herself. She watches his clever work with an artist's delight, and with the simple spirit of a child.

[17] When her father was created an earl in 1795, she became Lady Anne.

Nothing could be more distasteful to such a character than the affected pose of a woman of fashion. She has dropped into a chair with a careless grace all her own, and tells the painter she is ready. He takes up his brush, and lo, the very essence of her smile is transferred to his canvas. [75]

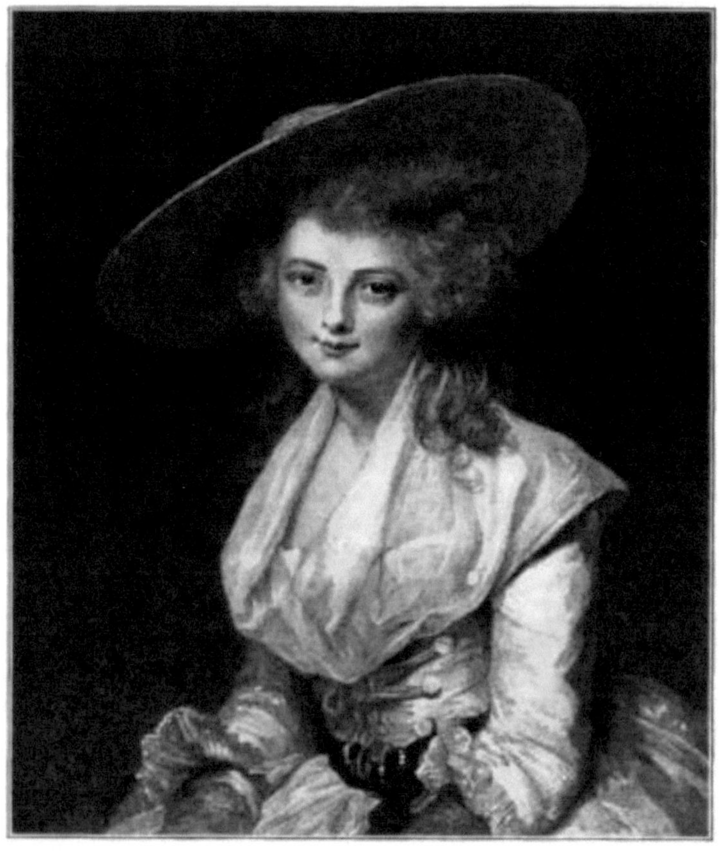

THE HON. ANNE BINGHAM

Please click on the image for a larger image.

Please click here for a modern color image

[77]

We praise the delicate rendering of the gauzy kerchief veiling her neck, but it is far less wonderful than the delicate interpretation of her expression. The fine sensitiveness of her nature, her lively fancy and sense of humor, her playfulness, her coquetry, her impulsiveness, her volatile temperament — all this we read in the shining eyes and the smiling mouth, though no one can say how they were made to tell so much. The signs of her birth and breeding are in every line, yet she is something of a Bohemian too. There is a delightful sense of camaraderie in her smile.

There is a certain portrait by Leonardo da Vinci known as the Mona Lisa, and famous for its baffling smile. There is a tantalizing quality about it which makes one forever wonder what the lady is thinking about and why she is smiling. Nothing could be more in contrast than this smile of Miss Bingham. There is no mystery in it, but rather it takes us into her confidence in the most winning way.

The costume interests us not only as a reminder of bygone fashions, but for its picturesqueness. The bodice is ornamented only by the big buttons by which it is laced. A narrow belt finishes it at the waist, with a small buckle in front.

The hair is frizzed in puffy masses about the face, escaping in a few curls which fall over the shoulders. This was evidently the favorite coiffure in the year 1786, as the portrait of the Duchess of Devonshire with her Child, painted in the same year, shows precisely the same style. Both ladies also wear low-cut [78] bodices with kerchiefs arranged in the same manner. The finishing touch of Miss Bingham's costume is the big straw hat worn aslant on the back of the head.

It has been a favorite device of great portrait painters to dress their sitters in all sorts of fanciful headwear. Rembrandt's portraits show an endless variety of caps, turbans, and hats. Rubens was fond of painting broad-brimmed hats shading the face, one of his celebrated pictures being a study of this kind called Le Chapeau de Paille (The Straw Hat).

Now Reynolds was to some extent an imitator of these two men, and it may be he learned something from their pictures about hats. However that may be, we see how the hat here proves very effective in bringing the head into harmonious relation with the whole composition. The brim describes a diagonal line parallel with the line made by the kerchief over the left shoulder. The kerchief on the right shoulder falls in a line parallel with the left arm.

A composition based on short diagonal lines like these is as different as possible in character from one of long flowing curves like Hope. Each one is appropriate to its own subject.

[79]

XIV

THE STRAWBERRY GIRL

Village life in England before the time of railroads had a picturesque charm which it has since lost except in remote districts. We learn something about it in Miss Mitford's sketches of "Our Village" and in Miss Edgeworth's "Tales." From such books it is delightful to reconstruct in imagination some of these rural scenes; the wide meadows where the cowslips grow, the brooks running beneath the hawthorns and alders, the lanes winding between hedgerows, the green common where the cricketers play, the low cottages covered to the roof with vines, and the trim gardens gay with pinks and larkspur. These villages are connected with the outside world only by the postcart and chapman. Here modest little girls like Miss Mitford's Hannah and Miss Edgeworth's Simple Susan move about their daily tasks and run on their errands of mercy.

Now Sir Joshua Reynolds was a native of Devonshire, a beautiful English district which all born Devons love with peculiar devotion, as we may see from Charles Kingsley's descriptions in "Waterbabies." From time to time in his busy life the painter returned to his home for a breath of country air. On one of these visits he brought back to [80] London with him his young niece Theophila Palmer, whose father had just died. Offy, as she was called, soon became the pet of her bachelor uncle's household, of which she long remained a member. As she flitted about the house the little country-bred girl with her fresh healthy beauty was a constant reminder to the painter of the woods and fields. Perhaps one day as he was looking at her with special pleasure the picture suddenly flashed upon his fancy of

Offy in the character of a village maid. The idea developed into the Strawberry Girl, for which Offy sat as model.

A little girl has been sent on an errand along a lonely road leading out of the village. It may be that like little Red Riding Hood in the nursery tale she is carrying some dainties to her grandmother. A basket of strawberries hangs on her arm, and her apron also seems to be filled with something, for it is gathered up in front like a bag, the corners dropping over the arm.

Twilight begins to fall as she comes to a turn of the road overshadowed by a high rock. There are all sorts of queer noises and shadows here, and she steals timidly past the eerie place, peering forward with big eyes.

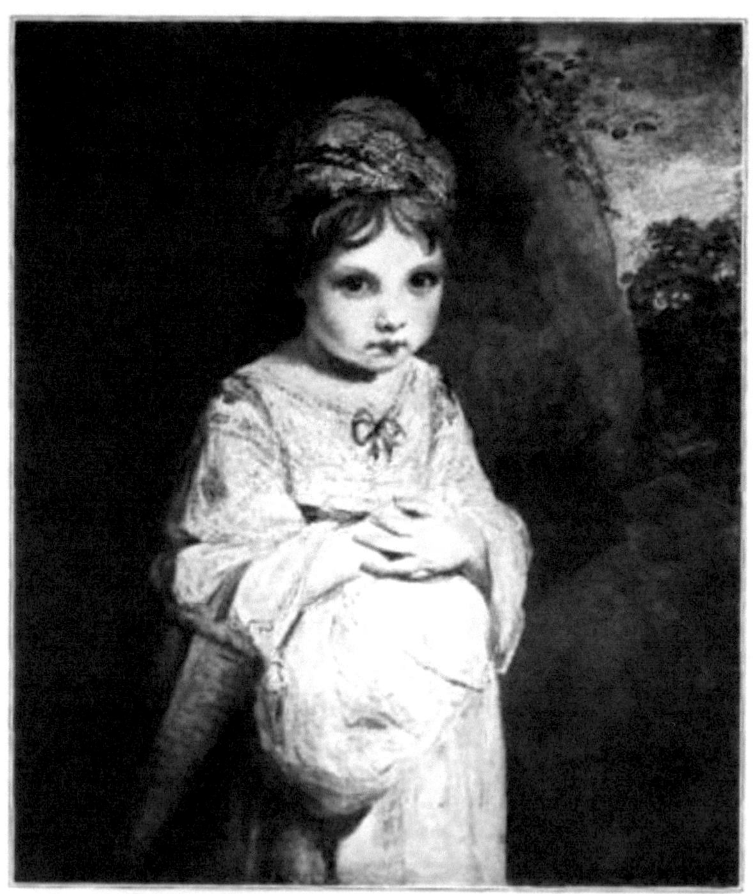

THE STRAWBERRY GIRL

Please click on the image for a larger image.

Please click here for a modern color image

Yet she is a womanly child, who will not easily be turned back. She feels the importance of her errand, and is worthy of the trust. The simple low-cut gown is that of a village maid. An odd cap, something like a turban, covers her head and adds a trifle to her height and dignity. Her round face [83] and chubby neck would be the envy of the puny city child who knows not the luxury of big porringers of bread and milk. If her hands are rather too delicately moulded for those of a country child we must remember again that Reynolds was painting from his own little niece.

In imagination we follow the little maid about the simple round of her childish pursuits. Every morning she goes demurely to school to fix her thoughts on "button holes and spelling books." Perhaps it is a dame school like that in "Water Babies," with a "shining clean stone floor and curious old prints on the wall and a cuckoo clock in the corner," Here some dozen children sit on benches "gabbling Chris-cross," while a nice old woman in a red petticoat and white cap hears them from the chimney corner.

Our little girl has duties at home as well, and is sometimes seen, a pitcher in one hand and a mop in the other, making the house tidy. She can boil potatoes, shell the beans, feed the hens, and make herself useful in many ways.

On rare occasions she has a holiday in the fields, and then what joy it is in spring and early summer to find the haunts of the wild flowers which grow in such abundance in the English country. Miss Mitford writes of a wonderful field where bloomed in season, "primroses, yellow, purple, and white, violets of either hue, cowslips, oxlips, arums, orchises, wild hyacinths, ground ivy, pansies, strawberries, and heart's ease, covering the sunny open slope under a weeping birch." [84]

A favorite game is making cowslip balls. The tufts of golden flowerets are first nipped off with short stems, until a quantity are gathered. Then the ribbon is held ready and the clusters are nicely balanced across it until a long garland is made, when they are pressed closely together and tied into a sweet golden ball.

When we remember that the little Offy, who was the original Strawberry Girl, was transplanted from her Devonshire home to the great city of London, we are interested to know something of her after life. She grew to be as dear as a daughter to her uncle. In the dreary days when he could not use his eyes she was his reader and amanuensis. The many distinguished guests who enjoyed his hospitality were charmed with her sweet manners. In the course of time she married Richard Lovell Gwatkin, a Cornish gentleman in every way worthy of her. "Her happiness was as great as her uncle could wish. She lived to be ninety, to see her children's children, and, intelligent, cheerful, and affectionate to the last, vividly remembered her happy girlhood under her uncle's roof, and the brilliant society that found a centre there."

[85]

XV

DR. SAMUEL JOHNSON

The eccentric figure of Dr. Samuel Johnson was one of the familiar sights of London during the middle of the eighteenth century. He was a man of great learning, a voluminous writer, and an even more remarkable talker. He was born in 1709, and, the son of a poor bookseller, he struggled against poverty for many years. Literary work was ill paid in those days, and Johnson gained his reputation but slowly. He contributed articles to the magazines, and twice he conducted short-lived periodicals of his own—the "Rambler" and the "Idler." He wrote, besides, a drama, "Irene"; a tale, "Rasselas"; a book of travel, a "Journey to the Hebrides"; and many biographies, including the "Lives of the Poets." His largest undertaking was an English dictionary, upon which he spent eight years of labor.

At length his pecuniary troubles came to an end when, in 1762, the government awarded him a pension of £300 a year. By this time his great intellectual gifts had begun to be appreciated, and he was the first man of letters in England. In Thackeray's phrase, he "was revered as a sort of oracle."

Johnson was now too old to acquire the graces of polite society, even had he wished them. His huge, [86] uncouth figure and rolling walk, his countenance disfigured by scrofula, his blinking eyes, his convulsive movements, his slovenly dress and boorish manners made him a strange figure in the circles which entertained him.

His appetite was enormous, and he ate "like a famished wolf, the veins swelling on his forehead, and the perspiration running down his cheeks." He usually declined wine, but his capacity for tea was unlimited. Many funny stories are told of the number of cups poured for him by obliging hostesses, for, oddly enough, he was a great favorite with the ladies, and knew how to turn a pretty compliment. His temper was at times very irritable and morbid, and he occasionally had violent fits of rage. Yet, with all these peculiarities, he had a kind heart and was sincerely religious. His devotion to his wife and his aged mother [18] was very touching, and the poor and infirm knew his charities. In his own lodgings he provided a home for an oddly assorted family of dependents, consisting of an old man, a blind woman, a negro boy, and a cat. All the details of his daily life and habits are minutely described in a biography written by his admiring friend, Boswell, who was intimately associated with him for many years. The book he wrote after Johnson's death tells us not only all about the learned doctor, but much also about his friends.

[18] His wife died in 1752, and his mother in 1759 at the age of ninety.

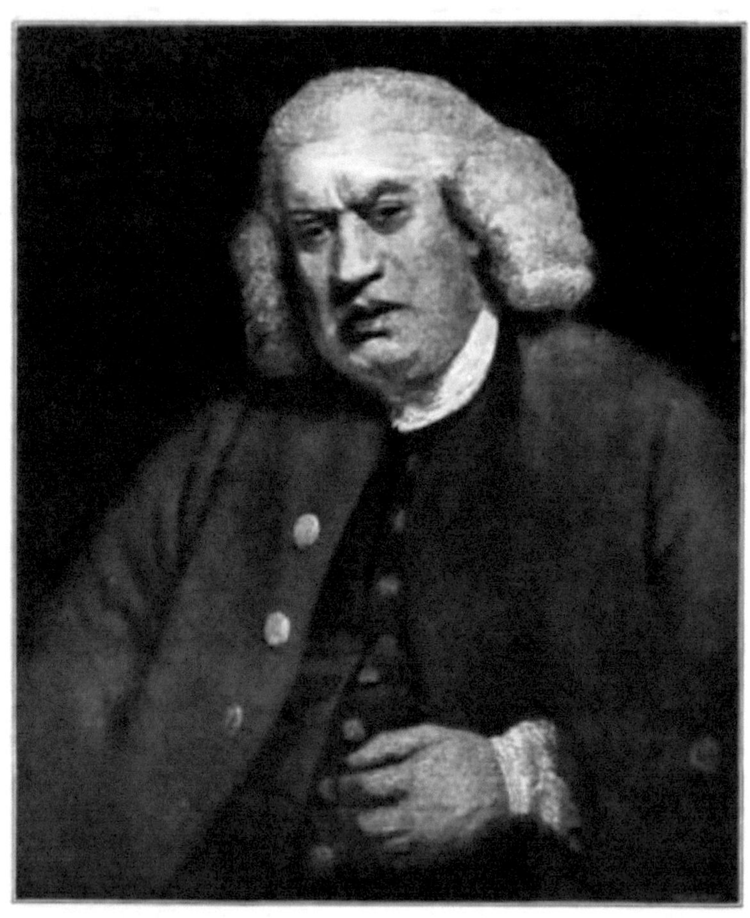

DR. SAMUEL JOHNSON

Please click on the image for a larger image.

Please click here for a modern color image

Reynolds was one of his warm friends, and the [88] two understood each other well. Often when they were together in company,
the painter's tact and courtesy smoothed over some breach of eti-
quette on the part of his companion. At Reynolds's suggestion, the
two founded together a small club of congenial spirits, called the
Literary Club.

Some other good friends of Johnson's were the Thrales. Mr. Thrale was a rich brewer, and a man of parts, and his wife was one of the brightest women of her day. Johnson was a constant visitor at their house, and became at last, practically, a member of the family. The Thrales's drawing-room at their Streatham villa was the scene of many brilliant gatherings, where intellectual people met for conversation and discussion. Johnson was the autocrat of this circle. He was often rude, even insolent, in expressing his opinion, and wounded many by his sarcasm. But his vast stores of information, his keen mind and ready wit, made his conversation an intellectual feast.

It was an ambition of Mr. Thrale to ornament his house with a gallery of portraits of contemporary celebrities, and it was for this collection that Reynolds painted the portrait of Johnson, reproduced in our illustration. It was really a repetition of a portrait he had previously painted for their common friend and club-fellow, Bennet Langton.

Here we see the sage at the age of sixty odd years, precisely as he appeared among his friends at Streatham. The painter has straightened the wig, which was usually worn awry, but otherwise it is the [90] very Dr. Johnson of whom we read so much, with his shabby brown coat, his big shambling shoulders, and coarse features.

A remarkable thing about the portrait is that Reynolds succeeded so well in showing us the man himself under this rough exterior. The inferior artist paints only the outside of a face just as it looks to a stranger who knows nothing of the character of the sitter. The master paints the face as it looks to a friend who knows the soul within. Now, Reynolds was not only a master, but he was, in this case, painting a friend. So he put on the canvas, not merely the eccentric face of Dr. Johnson as a stranger might see it, but he painted in it that expression of intellectual power which the great man showed among his congenial friends. Something, too, is suggested in the portrait of that sternly upright spirit which hated a lie.

It is a portrait of Johnson the scholar, the thinker, and the conversationalist. He seems to be engaged in some argument, and is delivering his opinion with characteristic authoritativeness. The heavy features are lighted by his thought. One may fancy that the talk turns upon patriotism, when Johnson, roused to indignation by the false pretences of many would-be patriots, exclaims, "Sir, patriotism is the last refuge of a scoundrel."

[91]

XVI

THE PORTRAIT OF REYNOLDS

In the city of Florence, Italy, there is a famous gallery of portraits unlike any other collection of pictures in the world. It consists of the portraits of artists, painted by their own hands, and includes the most celebrated painters of all nations, from the fifteenth century to the present time. Here may be seen the portraits of Velasquez, Titian, Tintoretto, Rembrandt,—the world's greatest portrait painters,—and in the same splendid company hangs the portrait of Reynolds, reproduced in our frontispiece. He painted it in 1776 for the special purpose of sending it to Florence at the request of the Imperial Academy of that city, of which he had just been elected a member.

As we have seen in our study of the Angels' Heads, a single portrait can show us only one side of the sitter's character. This portrait of Reynolds, painted as a condition of membership in a society of artists, and for a gallery of artists' portraits, was intended chiefly to show the artistic side of his nature. The pose itself at once suggests the artist. The expression of the mobile face is that of a painter engaged at his easel, turning a searching glance upon the object he is painting. In short, it is a sort [92] of official portrait, introducing the new member to his associates in the Imperial Academy.

The artist wears the Oxford cap and gown, to which he is entitled, by virtue of the honorary degree of D. C. L., conferred upon him by the University of Oxford. In his hand he carries a roll of manuscript, presumably one of his lectures before the Royal Academy. Both the roll and the costume are, as it were, insignia of his English honors. A Latin inscription on the back of the portrait, written by the painter's own hand, enumerates the several distinctions which are his.

Reynolds might, indeed, be pardoned the pride with which he reviewed his career. From somewhat humble beginnings he had now made his way to the foremost place in his profession. He was born at a time when art was in a very low state in England, and there were no advantages for the study of painting. His only instruction was under an inferior portrait painter named Hudson, with whom he served as apprentice about two years.

His real art training was during three years of travel in Italy. There he examined and studied the works of the greatest masters of the past, and returned to England with altogether new ideals. Setting up a studio in London, he soon gained an immense popularity. When the Royal Academy was founded, in 1768, he became the first president, and at the same time the honor of knighthood was conferred upon him. Other artists now rose to prominence, but he still held the supremacy. [93]

The painter's popularity depended by no means on his artistic talents alone; his opinions were worth hearing on many subjects. He was fond of books and literary discussions, and his friendship was valued by such men of intellect as Johnson, Goldsmith, Burke, and others of that charmed circle making the Literary Club. He had a genial, kindly nature, and his manners were exquisitely courteous. Thackeray once wrote that "of all the polite men of that age, Joshua Reynolds was the finest gentleman." He was a member of several clubs, was fond of society, and was a welcome guest in many of the best houses in London. He himself entertained with generous hospitality, and gathered about his table some of the brightest people of his time.

His intimate friend, Edmund Malone, described him as a man "rather under the middle size, of a florid complexion, and a lively and pleasing aspect; well made, and extremely active. His appearance at first sight impressed the spectator with the idea of a well-born and well-bred English gentleman. With an uncommon equability of temper, which, however, never degenerated into insipidity or apathy, he possessed a constant flow of spirits which rendered him at all times a most pleasing companion.... He appeared to me the happiest man I have ever known."

Through many years Reynolds was very deaf, and was obliged to use an ear trumpet to aid him in general conversation. In later years he also wore spectacles, so that we always picture him in his [94] advancing life with trumpet and glasses. His habit of taking great quantities of snuff was one which gave occasion to many jokes among his friends.

Numerous poetic tributes were written by his admirers, describing more or less rhetorically his qualities as a man and an artist. There is one bit of verse by Goldsmith (1770), in a comic vein, and in the form of an epitaph, which delineates very cleverly the real character of the man: —

> "Here Reynolds is laid, and to tell you my mind,
> He has not left a better or wiser behind;
> His pencil was striking, resistless and grand,
> His manners were gentle, complying, and bland;
> Still born to improve us in every part,
> His pencil, our faces, his manners, our heart:
> To coxcombs averse, yet most civilly steering,
> When they judged without skill, he was still hard of hearing;
> When they talked of their Raffaelles, Correggios, and stuff,
> He shifted his trumpet, and only took snuff!"